1,000,000 Books

are available to read at

www.ForgottenBooks.com

Read online
Download PDF
Purchase in print

ISBN 978-0-259-20153-3
PIBN 10809510

This book is a reproduction of an important historical work. Forgotten Books uses state-of-the-art technology to digitally reconstruct the work, preserving the original format whilst repairing imperfections present in the aged copy. In rare cases, an imperfection in the original, such as a blemish or missing page, may be replicated in our edition. We do, however, repair the vast majority of imperfections successfully; any imperfections that remain are intentionally left to preserve the state of such historical works.

Forgotten Books is a registered trademark of FB &c Ltd.
Copyright © 2018 FB &c Ltd.
FB &c Ltd, Dalton House, 60 Windsor Avenue, London, SW19 2RR.
Company number 08720141. Registered in England and Wales.

For support please visit www.forgottenbooks.com

1 MONTH OF FREE READING

at

www.ForgottenBooks.com

By purchasing this book you are eligible for one month membership to ForgottenBooks.com, giving you unlimited access to our entire collection of over 1,000,000 titles via our web site and mobile apps.

To claim your free month visit: www.forgottenbooks.com/free809510

* Offer is valid for 45 days from date of purchase. Terms and conditions apply.

English
Français
Deutsche
Italiano
Español
Português

www.forgottenbooks.com

Mythology Photography **Fiction** Fishing Christianity **Art** Cooking Essays **Buddhism** Freemasonry Medicine **Biology** Music **Ancient Egypt** Evolution Carpentry Physics Dance Geology **Mathematics** Fitness Shakespeare **Folklore** Yoga Marketing **Confidence** Immortality Biographies Poetry **Psychology** Witchcraft Electronics Chemistry History **Law** Accounting **Philosophy** Anthropology Alchemy Drama Quantum Mechanics Atheism Sexual Health **Ancient History** **Entrepreneurship** Languages Sport Paleontology Needlework Islam **Metaphysics** Investment Archaeology Parenting Statistics Criminology **Motivational**

A Practical Discourse

CONCERNING

DEATH.

By WILLIAM SHERLOCK, D.D.
Late Dean of St. *Paul's*.

The Seven and Twentieth Edition.

LONDON:
Printed for R. WARE, J. WALTHOE, J. and
P. KNAPTON, S. BIRT, D. BROWNE,
T. LONGMAN, C. HITCH and L. HAWES,
J. CLARKE, J. HODGES, J. HINTON, J. and
J. RIVINGTON, R. BALDWIN, and J. WARD.

MDCCLI.

THE NEW YORK
PUBLIC LIBRARY
588724
ASTOR, LENOX AND
TILDEN FOUNDATIONS.
R 1913 L

To the Worshipful the
Masters of the Bench,

And the rest of the

Members of the Two Honourable Societies

OF THE

TEMPLE.

My much honoured Friends,

ONE Reason of Publishing this plain Discourse is, because I cannot now preach to you as formerly I have done, and have no other Way left of discharging my Duty to you, but by making the Press supply the Place of the Pulpit. Part of this you have already heard, and should have heard the rest, had I enjoyed the same Liberty still; which God restore to me again when he sees fit; if not, his Will be done.

And the only Reason of this Dedication is, to make this publick and thankful Acknowledgment (before I am forced

The Epistle Dedicatory.

ced from you, if I must be so unhappy) of your great Respects, and many singular Favours to me; which have been always so free and generous, that they never gave Time, nor left any Room for me to ask; especially that obliging Welcome you gave me at my first Coming, I mean your Present of a House, which, besides the Conveniencies and Pleasure of a delightful Habitation, has afforded me that which I value much more, the frequent Opportunities of your Conversation.

Tho' I am able to make you no better Return than Thanks, I hope that Great MASTER whom I serve will; and that GOD would multiply all temporal and spiritual Blessings on you, is, and always shall be, the sincere and hearty Prayer of,

GENTLEMEN,

Your most Obliged,

and Humble Servant,

W. SHERLOCK.

THE CONTENTS.

THE *Introduction,* Page 1

CHAP. I.

The several Notions of Death; and the Improvement of them, 3

SECT. I. *The first Notion of Death, That it is our leaving this World; with the Improvement of it,* 5

SECT. II. *The Second Notion of Death, That it is our putting off these Bodies,* 29

SECT. III. *Death considered as our Entrance upon a new and unknown State of Life,* 57

CHAP. II.

Concerning the Certainty of our Death, 74

SECT. I. *A Vindication of the Justice and Goodness of God, in appointing Death for all Men,* 75

SECT. II. *How to improve this Consideration, That we must certainly die,* 91

CHAP. III.

Concerning the Time of our Death, and the proper Improvement of it, 104

SECT.

CONTENTS.

Sect. I. *That the general Period of human Life is fixed and determined by God, and that it is but very short,* Page 106

Sect. II. *What little Reason we have to complain of the Shortness of human Life,* 111

Sect. III. *What Use to make of the fixed Term of human Life,* 119

Sect. IV. *What Use to make of the Shortness of human Life,* 133

Sect. V. *The Time and Manner, and Circumstances of every particular Man's Death, are not determined by an absolute and unconditional Decree,* 152

Sect. VI. *The particular Time when we are to die is unknown and uncertain to us,* 161

Sect. VII. *That we must die but once, or that Death translates us to an unchangeable State; with the Improvement of it,* 193

CHAP. IV.

Concerning the Fear of Death and the Remedies against it, 272

The Conclusion, 291

TO
Dr. *SHERLOCK,*
ON
His Discourse concerning *DEATH.*

FORGIVE the Muse, who, in unhallow'd Strains,
　　The Saint one Moment from his GOD detains.
　　For sure whate'er you do, whate'er you are,
'Tis all but one good Work, one constant Prayer.
Forgive her; and intreat that GOD to whom
Thy favour'd Vows with kind Acceptance come,
To raise her Notes to that sublime Degree,
That suits a Song of Piety and Thee.

　Wond'rous good Man! whose Labours may repel
The Force of Sin, may stop the Rage of Hell:
Who, like the *Baptist*, from thy GOD was sent
The crying Voice to bid the World repent.

　Thee Youth shall study; and no more engage
His flattering Wishes for uncertain Age;
No more, with fruitless Care, and cheated Strife,
Chase fleeting Pleasure through this Maze of Life;

Finding

Finding the wretched All he here can have;
But present Food, and but a future Grave;
Each, great as *Philip*'s Victor Son, shall view
This abject World, and weeping ask a New.

Decrepit Age shall read thee, and confess
Thy Labours can assuage where Med'cines cease:
Shall bless thy Words, their wounded Souls Relief;
The Drops that sweeten their last Dregs of Life;
Shall look to Heav'n, and laugh at all beneath;
Own Riches gather'd, Trouble; Fame, a Breath;
And Life, an Ill, whose only Cure is Death.

Thy even Thoughts with so much Plainness flow,
Their Sense untutor'd Infancy may know;
Yet to such Height is all that Plainness wrought,
Wit may admire, and letter'd Pride be taught.
Easy in Words thy Style, in Sense sublime;
On its blest Steps each Age and Sex may rise:
'Tis like the Ladder in the Patriarch's Dream,
Its Foot on Earth, its Height beyond the Skies.
Diffus'd its Virtue, boundless is its Pow'r;
'Tis publick Health, and universal Cure.
Of heavenly Manna 'tis a second Feast,
A Nation's Food, and all to ev'ry Taste.

To its last Height mad *Britain*'s Guilt was rear'd:
And various Deaths for various Crimes she fear'd;
With your kind Work her drooping Hopes revive,
You bid her read, repent, adore, and live.
You wrest the Bolt from Heaven's avenging Hand;
Stop ready Death, and save a sinking Land.

O!

O! save us still, still bless us with thy Stay;
O! want thy Heav'n, 'till we have learnt the Way;
Refuse to leave thy destin'd Charge too soon;
And for the Church's Good, defer thy own:
O! live, and let thy Works urge our Belief;
Live to explain thy Doctrine by thy Life;
'Till future Infancy, baptiz'd by thee,
Grow ripe in Years, and old in Piety;
'Till Christians yet unborn be taught to die.

Then in full Age, and hoary Holiness,
Retire, great Teacher, to thy promis'd Bliss:
Untouch'd thy Tomb, uninjur'd be thy Dust,
As thy own Fame among the future Just;
'Till in last Sounds the dreaded Trumpet speaks;
'Till Judgment calls, and quicken'd Nature wakes;
'Till through the utmost Earth and deepest Sea,
Our scatter'd *Atoms* find their destin'd Way;
In haste to cloath their Kindred Souls again,
Perfect our State, and build immortal Man:
Then fearless, Thou, who well sustain'd the Fight,
To Paths of Joy, and Tracks of endless Light,
Lead up all those, that heard thee, and believ'd:
'Midst thy own Flock, great Shepherd, be receiv'd;
And glad all Heav'n with Millions thou hast sav'd.

A

A

Practical Discourse

CONCERNING

DEATH.

HEB. ix. 27.
It is appointed unto all men once to die.

The INTRODUCTION.

HERE is not a more effectual Way to revive the true Spirit of Christianity in the World, than seriously to meditate on what we commonly call the Four last THINGS, Death, Judgment, Heaven, and Hell; for it is morally impossible Men should live such careless Lives, should so wholly devote themselves to this World, and the Service of their Lusts; should

either

either cast off the Fear of God, and all Reverence for his Laws, to satisfy themselves with some cold and formal Devotions, were they possessed with a warm and constant Sense of these Things. For what manner of Men ought we to be, who know that we must shortly die, and come to Judgment, and receive according to what we have done in this World, whether it be Good or Evil, either eternal Rewards in the Kingdom of Heaven, or eternal Punishments with the Devil and his Angels?

That which first presents itself to our Thoughts, and shall be the Subject of this following Treatise, is DEATH; a very terrible Thing, the very naming of which is apt to chill our Blood and Spirits, and to draw a dark Veil over all the Glories of this Life. And yet this is the Condition of all Mankind, we must as surely die, as we are born: *For it is appointed unto men once to die.* This is not the Original Law of our Nature; for though Man was made of the Dust of the Earth, and therefore was by Nature mortal; (for that which is made of Dust is by Nature corruptible, and may be resolved into Dust again) yet had he not sinned, he should never have died; he should have been immortal by Grace, and therefore had the Sacrament of Immortality, the Tree of Life, planted in Paradise: But now *by man sin entered into the world, and death by sin; and so death passed upon all men, for that all have sinned,* Rom. v. 12. And thus it is decreed and appointed by God, by an irreversible Sentence, *Dust thou art, and unto dust thou shalt return.*

Now to improve this Meditation to the best Advantage, I shall, 1. Consider what Death is, and what Wisdom that should teach us. 2. The Certainty of our Death, That *it is appointed unto men once to die.* 3. The Time of our Death; it must be once, but when, we know not. 4. The natural Fears and Terrors of Death, or our natural Aversion to it, and how they may be allayed and sweetened.

CHAP. I.

The several Notions of Death, and the Improvement of them.

1. WHAT Death is: And I shall consider three Things in it: 1. That it is our leaving this World. 2. Our putting off these earthly Bodies. 3. Our Entrance into a new and unknown State of Life; for when we die, we do not fall into nothing, or into a profound Sleep, into a Sate of Silence and Insensibility 'till the Resurrection; but we only change our Place, and our Dwelling; we remove out of this World, and leave our Bodies to sleep in the Earth 'till the Resurrection, but our Souls and Spirits still live in an invisible State. I shall not go about to

prove these Things, but take it for granted that you all believe them; for that we leave this World, and that our Bodies rot and putrify in the Grave, needs no Proof, for we see it with our Eyes; and that our Souls cannot die, but are by Nature immortal, has been the Belief of all Mankind. The Gods which the Heathens worshipped, were most of them no other but dead Men; and therefore they did believe that the Soul survived the Funeral of the Body, or they could never have made Gods of them: Nay, there is such a strong Sense of Immortality imprinted in our Natures, that very few Men, how much soever they have debauched their natural Sentiments, can wholly deliver themselves from the Fears of another World. But we have a more sure Word of Prophecy than this: Since *life and immortality is brought to light by the Gospel.* For this is so plainly taught in Scripture, that no Man who believes that, needs any other Proof. My Business therefore shall only be to shew you how such Thoughts as these should affect our Minds: What that Wisdom is, which the Thoughts of Death will naturally teach us; how that Man ought to live, who knows that he must die, and leave his Body behind him to rot in the Grave, and go himself into a new World of Spirits.

S. E C T.

SECT. I.

The first Notion of Death, That it is our Leaving this World; with the Improvement of it.

I. FIRST then, let us consider Death only as our leaving this World; a very delightful Place, you'll say, especially when our Circumstances are easy and prosperous: Here a Man finds whatever he most naturally loves, whatever he takes Pleasure in; the Supply of all his Wants, the Gratification of all his Senses, whatever an earthly Creature can wish for or desire. The Truth is, few Men know any other Happiness, much less any thing above it. They feel what strikes upon their Senses: This they think a real and substantial Good; but as for more pure and intellectual Joys, they know no more what to make of them than of Ghosts and Spirits; they account them thin vanishing Things, and wonder what Men mean who talk so much of them. Nay, good Men themselves are apt to be too much pleased with this World, while they are easy here; something else is necessary to wean them from it, and to cure their Fondness of it, besides the Thoughts of Dying; which makes the Sufferings and Afflictions, and Disappointments of this Life, so necessary for the best of Men. This is one Thing which makes the Thoughts of Death so terrible: Men think themselves very well as they are, and moſt Men think that they cannot be better, and therefore very few are deſirous of a Change. Extreme Miſeries may conquer the Love of Life, and ſome few Divine Souls may long with St *Paul* to be diſſolved and to be with Chriſt, which is beſt of all; but this World is a beloved Place to the Generality of Mankind, and that makes it a very troubleſome thing to leave it: Whereas did we rightly conſider this Matter, it would rectify our Miſtakes about theſe Things, and teach us how to value, and how to uſe them. For,

1. If we muſt leave this World, how valuable ſoever theſe Things are in themſelves, they are not ſo valuable to us. For beſides the intrinſick Worth of Things, there is ſomething more required to engage the Affections of wiſe Men; *viz.* Propriety, and a ſecure Enjoyment. What is not our own, we may admire if it be excellent, but cannot doat on; and what is worth having Increaſes or Decreaſes in Value, proportionable to the Length and Certainty of its Continuance: What we cannot enjoy is nothing to us, how excellent ſoever it be; and to enjoy it but a little while is next to not enjoying it, for we cannot enjoy it always; and ſuch Things cannot be called our own. And this ſhews us what Value we ought to ſet upon this World, and all Things in it; e'en juſt ſo much as upon Things that are not our own, and which we cannot keep.

We uſe indeed to call Things our own, which we have a legal Title to, which no Man can

can by Law or Justice deprive us of; and this is the only Property we can have in these Things, a Property against all other human Claims: But nothing which can be taken from us, nothing which we must leave, is properly our own; for in a strict Sense nothing is our own, but what is essential either to our Being, or to our Happiness. Creatures are Proprietors of nothing, not so much as of themselves; for we are his who made us, and may unmake us again when he pleases: But yet there are some Things proper to our Natures, and that is all the natural Property we have; but what is thus proper to us, we cannot be deprived of, without ceasing to be, or being miserable.

And this proves that the Things of this World are not our own, that they are not proper and peculiar to our Natures, tho' they are necessary to this present State of Life. While we live here we want them, but when we leave this World, we must live without them, and may be happy without them too. There is a great Agreeableness between the Things of this World, and an earthly Nature; they are a great Support and Comfort to us in this mortal State; and therefore while we live in this World we may value the Enjoyments of it, for the Ease and Conveniencies of Life; but we must neither call this Life, nor any Enjoyments of it, our own, because they are short and perishing. We are here but as Travellers in an Inn; it it not our Home and Country, it is not our Portion and Inheritance, but a moveable and changeable Scene, which is entertaining at present, but cannot last. Let us then consider how we ought to value such Things as these: And to make it as plain and self-evident as I can, I shall put some easy and familiar Cases.

1. Suppose you were travelling thro' a very delightful Country, where you met with all the Pleasures and Conveniencies of Life, but knew that you must not tarry there, but only pass thro' it: Would you think it reasonable to set your Affections so much upon it, as to make it uneasy to you to leave it? And shall we then grow so fond of this World, which we must only pass thro', where we have no abiding City, as to enslave ourselves to the Lusts and Pleasures of it, and to carry out of this World such a Passion for it, as shall make us miserable in the next? For tho' Death will separate us from this World, we are not sure it will cure our earthly Passions: We may still find the Torment of sensual Appetites, when all sensual Objects are removed. This was all the Purgatory-Fire St *Austin* could think of, that those who loved this World too much here, though otherwise innocent and virtuous Men, should be punished with fruitless Desires and Hankerings after this World in the next; which is a mixed Torment of Desire and Despair. For though indeed it is only living in these Bodies, which betrays the Soul to such earthly Affections; yet when the Impression is once made, and is strong and vigorous,

gorous, we are not sure that merely putting off these Bodies will cure it; as we see Age itself in old Sinners does not cure the Wantonness of Desire, when the Body is effete and languid: And this I should think were Reason enough to convince every Man, who considers that he is not to live here always, how much it concerns him not to grow over fond of present Things; for to contract an eternal Passion for what we cannot always enjoy, must needs make us miserable.

2. If then we must not entertain a Fondness for those Things which we cannot keep, let us in the next Place consider, how we must use those Things which we have but a present and momentary Possession of: For Use is apt to beget a Fondness. Suppose then, again, that in your Travels abroad, you pass thro' such a delightful Country; what is it that prevents your Fondness, but only considering that you are not at home, that you must not always see and enjoy what you now do? And therefore all the fine Things you meet with, you rather look upon as Curiosities to be remarked in Story, or to be tried by way of Experiment, or to be used for present Necessity, than as such Things which are to be enjoyed, which you know they are not. And did we use the World thus, we should never grow over fond of it. Those *who marry, would be as though they married not; and those who weep, as though they wept not; and those who rejoice, as though they rejoiced not; and those who use*
this

to do with anything to recommend the *fashion* of this or that way of Life. The World itself will not last long, though it will out-last us; but we are certain here but little a while, that we have no Reason to call it our Home, or to place our Enjoyment in it. It is an old and a good Distinction, that some Things are only for Use, and some Things for Enjoyment. The first we value only for their Use, the second we account our Happiness. Now it is certain, that what is transient and momentary can be only for Use, for Man is a miserable Creature, if what is his Happiness be not lasting; and a very foolish Creature, if he places his Happiness in what is not lasting. Now this should make a vast Difference in our Affections to Things. We cannot blame any Man who lets loose his Affections upon that which is his Happiness; for there neither can, nor ought to be, any Bounds set to our Desires or Enjoyment of our true Happiness; but what we account only for Use, we have no farther Concernment for, but only as it is of Use to us; and this confines our Desires and Affections to its Use: And were this the Measure of our Love to present Things, as it ought to be, we could not err, nor entertain any troublesome or vicious Passion for them. As for Instance: What is the natural Use of eating and drinking, but to repair the Decays of Nature, and preserve our Bodies in Health and Vigour? Now, as great Delicacies and Curiosities as there are

in

in Nature, both of Food and Liquors, if Men valued them only for their Use, they would never be guilty of Excess, nor grow so fond of them, as if they were only to eat and drink, and to judge of the Differences of Tastes. To value Things for their Use, is to value them no further than they are useful; and this is the only Value which is due to Things which we must leave; for they can be only for present Use: But when we come to place our Happiness, as all sensual Men do, in Things which are designed only for our Use, it both makes us extravagant in the Use of them, [which often proves a great Mischief to us in this World] and creates such an unnatural Passion for them, as they cannot answer; which makes them vain and empty, and unsatisfactory while we have them, and fills us with Vexation, and all the Restlessness of a furious Passion and Appetite when we want them; as we must do at one time or other, either before, or, to be sure, when we leave this World.

3. Let us suppose again, That in our Passage through foreign Countries, where we are not to stay long, we should not meet with all those Necessaries and Conveniencies of Life, which we have at Home; that the Country is barren, the Way rough and mountainous, the Road infested with Thieves and Robbers, but without any convenient Reception for Travellers, the People rude and barbarous, and insolent to Strangers; will a wise Man

be

be over-sollicitous about such Hardships as these in travelling? Does he not comfort himself, that he is not to stay there, that this will not last long; that these Difficulties will only recommend his own Country to him, and make him hasten Home again, where he shall remember with Pleasure, what is now uneasy and troublesome?

And is there not as much Reason for Christians to bear all the Evils, and Casualties, and Sufferings of this Life with an equal Mind, remembering that they are not to stay always here? That this Life is but their Pilgrimage, they are from Home, and therefore must expect the Usage which Strangers and Travellers ordinarily meet with. That they are not to live here always, is a sufficient Proof that their Happiness does not consist in present Things: And then if they can make a Shift, tho' may be it is a hard Shift, to pass thro' this World, the Scene will be altered, and they shall find a kinder Reception in the next. This is the Foundation of Contentment in all Conditions, and of Patience under Sufferings; That Death, which is not far off, when it removes us out of this World, will remove us from all the Sufferings of it: And why should we not bear up with the Courage and Resolution of Travellers in the mean Time, when we have Home, a peaceful and eternal Home, in our Prospect?

4. Once more, to conclude this Argument: Suppose a Man in his Travels through a foreign

reign Country should be commanded immediately to leave the Country, unless he would forswear ever returning to his own Country again; would not a wise Man consider, that if he had not been commanded to leave that Country, he did not intend to have stayed long in it; and therefore it would be an unaccountable Folly and Madness in him to abjure his own Country, where his Father, and Kindred, and Inheritance are, only to gratify his Curiosity in staying a little longer there? And can we then think it a hard Command, (when we know we must shortly die, and leave this World, that whether we will or no, we cannot stay long in it,) to sacrifice our very Lives, rather than renounce our Hopes of Heaven and a better Life? When we know that we must leave this World, what does it signify to die a little sooner than it may be in the Course of Nature we should, to obtain an immortal Life; to go to that blessed Jesus who lived in this World for us, and died for us, and is ready to receive us into that blessed Place where he is, that we may behold his Glory? I am sure it is a very foolish Thing for a Man who must die, to forfeit an immortal Life, to reprieve a mortal and perishing Life for some few Years.

II. As Death, which is our leaving this World, proves that these present Things are not very valuable to us, so it proves that they are not the most valuable Things in their own Natures; tho' we were to enjoy them always,

it

it would be but a very mean and imperfect State, in Comparison of that better Life which is reserved for good Men in the next World: For, 1. It is congruous to the divine Wisdom and Goodness, that the best Things should be the most lasting: Wisdom dictates this; for it is no more than to give the Preference to those Things which are best. The longest Continuance gives a natural Preference to Things; we always value those Things most, which we shall enjoy longest; and therefore to give the longest Duration to the worst Things, is to set the greatest Value on them, and to teach Mankind to prefer them before that which is better. What we value most, we desire to enjoy longest, and were it in our Power we would make such Things the most lasting; which shews that it is the natural Sense of Mankind, that the best Things deserve to continue longest; and therefore we need not doubt, but that infinite Wisdom which made the World, has proportioned the Continuance of Things to their true Worth. And if God has made the best Things the most lasting, then the next World in its own intrinsick Nature is as much better than this World, as it will last longer. For this is most agreeable to the Divine Goodness too, and God's Love to his Creatures, that what is their greatest and truest Happiness should be most lasting. For if God has made Man capable of different Degrees and States of Happiness, of living in this World and in the next, it is

an

an Expression of more perfect Goodness (as it is most for the Happiness of his Creatures) that the most perfect State of Happiness should last the longest; for the more perfectly happy we are, the more do we experience the Divine Goodness; and he is the most perfectly happy, who has the longest Enjoyment of the best Things.

2. It seems most agreeable also to the Divine Wisdom and Goodness, that where God makes such a vast Change in the State of his Creatures, as to remove them from this World to the next, the last State should be the most perfect and happy. I speak now of such Creatures as God designs for Happiness, for the Reason alters where he intends to punish. But where God intends to do good to Creatures, it seems a very impoper Method to translate them from a more perfect and happy, to a less happy State. Every Abatement of Happiness is a Degree of Punishment, and that which those Men are very sensible of, who have enjoyed a more perfect Happiness: And therefore we may certainly conclude, that God would not remove good Men out of this World, were this the happiest Place.

Yes, you'll say, Death is the Punishment of Sin, and therefore it is a Punishment to be removed out of this World; which spoils that Argument, that this World is not the happiest Place; because God removes good Men out of it: For this is the Effect of that Curse which

which was entailed on Mankind for the Sin of *Adam*, *Duſt thou art, and to Duſt thou ſhalt return.*

Now I grant, Death, as it ſignifies a Separation of Soul and Body, and the Death of both, which was included in that Curſe, was a Curſe and a Puniſhment, but not as it ſignifies leaving this World, and living in the next.

We have ſome Reaſon to think, that tho' Man ſhould never have died, if he had not ſinned, yet he ſhould not always have lived in this World. Human Nature was certainly made for greater Things than the Enjoyments of Senſe: It is capable of nobler Advancements, it is related to Heaven, and to the World of Spirits; and therefore it ſeems more likely, that had Man continued innocent, and by the conſtant Exerciſe of Wiſdom and Virtue improved his Faculties, and raiſed himſelf above this Body, and grown up into the Divine Nature and Life, after a long and happy Life here, he ſhould have been tranſlated into Heaven as *Enoch* and *Elias* were, without dying. For had all Men continued innocent, and lived to this Day, and propagated their Kind, this little Spot of Earth had many Ages ſince been over-peopled, and could not have ſubſiſted, without tranſplanting ſome Colonies of the moſt divine and purified Souls into the other World.

But however that be, it is certain, that being removed out of this World, and living in Heaven,

Heaven, is not the Curse: This fallen Man had no Right to; for he, who by Sin had forfeited an earthly Paradise, could not thereby gain a Title to Heaven. *Eternal life is the gift of God, through Jesus Christ our Lord*; it is the Reward of good Men, of a well-spent Life in this World, of our Faith and Patience in doing and suffering the Will of God; it is our last and final State, where we shall live for ever; and therefore the Argument is still good, that this World cannot be the happiest Place, for then Heaven could not be a Reward. Though all Men are under the Necessity of dying, yet if this World had been the happiest Place, God would have raised good Men to have lived again in this World; which he could as easily have done, as have translated them to Heaven.

Now if this World be not the happiest Place, if present Things be not the most valuable, as appears from this very Consideration, that we must leave this World, (for to this I must confine my Discourse at present) there are several very good Uses to be made of this: As, 1. To rectify our Notions about present Things. 2. To live in Expectation of some better Things. 3. Not to be overconcerned about the Shortness of our Lives here.

1. To rectify our Notions about present Things. 'Tis our Opinions of Things which ruin us: For what Mankind account their greatest Happiness, they must love, and they must

must love without Bounds and Measure: And it would go a great Way to cure our extravagant Fondness and Passion for these Things, could we persuade ourselves that there is any Thing better. But this, I confess, is a very hard Thing for most Men to do, because present Things have much the Advantage of what is absent and future. Some who believe another Life after this, whatever great Things they may talk of the other World, yet do not seem throroughly persuaded, that the next World is a happier State than this; for I think they could not be so fond of this World if they were: And the Reason of it is plain, because Happiness cannot be so well known, as by feeling; now Men feel the Pleasures and Happiness of this World, but do not feel the Happiness of the next; and therefore are apt to think, that that is the greatest Happiness, which does most sensibly affect them: But would they but seriously consider Things, they might see Reason to think otherwise; that the unknown Joys and Pleasures of the other World are much greater than any Pleasures which they feel here. For let us thus reason with ourselves: I find I am mortal, and must shortly leave this World; and yet I believe that my Soul cannot die as my Body does, but shall only be translated to another State; whatever I take Pleasure in, in this World, I must leave behind me, and know not what I shall find in the next: But surely the other World, where I must live for ever,

is

is not worse furnished than this World, which I must so quickly leave. For has God made me immortal, and provided no Sorts of Pleasures and Entertainments for an immortal State, when he has so liberally furnished the short and changeable Scene of this Life? I know not indeed what the Pleasures of the next World are; but no more did I know what the Pleasures of this World were till I came into it; and therefore, that is no Argument that there are no Pleasures there, because I do not yet know them. And if there be any Pleasures there, surely there must be greater than what are here, because it is a more lasting State. For can we think, that God has emptied all his Stores and Treasures into this World? Nay, can we think that he has given the best Things first, where we can only just taste them, and leave them behind us? Which is to excite and provoke an Appetite, which shall be restless and uneasy to Eternity. No, surely! the other World must be infinitely a more happy Place than this, because it will last infinitely longer. The Divine Wisdom and Goodness has certainly reserv'd the best Things for Eternity: For as eternal Beings are the most perfect, so they must be the most happy too, unless we can separate Perfection and Happiness. And therefore I cannot but conclude, that there are greater Pleasures, that there is a happier State of Life than this, because there is a Life which lasts for ever.

2. This will naturally teach us to live in Expectation of better Things, of greater, tho' unknown and unexperienced Pleasures; which methinks all Men should do, who know that there are better Things to be had, and that they must go into that State where these better Things are to be had. For, can any Man be contented with a less Degree of Happiness, who knows there is greater? This is Stupidity and Baseness of Spirit; an ignoble Mind, which is not capable of great Hopes. Ambition and Covetousness indeed are ill Names, but yet they are Symptoms of a great and generous Soul, and are excellent Virtues, when directed to the right Objects; that is, to such Objects as are truly great and excellent; for it is only the Meanness of the Object which makes them Vices. To be ambitious of true Honour, of the true Glory and Perfection of our Natures is the very Principle and Incentive of Virtue: but to be ambitious of Titles, of Place, of some ceremonious Respects, and civil Pageantry, is as vain and little, as the Things are which they court. To be covetous of true and real Happiness, to set no Bounds nor Measures to our Desire or Pursuit of it, is true Greatness of Mind, which will take up with nothing on this Side Perfection: For God and Nature have set no Bounds to our Desires and Happiness; but as it is in natural, so it it ought to be in moral, Agents, every Thing grows till it comes to it's Maturity and Perfection. But then
Covetousness

Covetousness is a Vice, when Men mistake their Object, and are insatiable in their Desires of that which is not their Happiness; as Gold and Silver, Houses and Land; what is more than we want, and more than we can use, cannot be the Happiness of a Man. And thus it is on the other Hand; tho' Humility be a great Virtue, as it is opposed to earthly Ambitions, as it sets us above the little Opinions and Courtship of the World, which are such mean Things, as argue Meanness of Spirit to stoop to them; yet it is not Humility but Sordidness, to be regardless of true Honour. Thus, to be contented with our external Fortune in this World, whatever it be; to be able to see the greater Prosperity and Splendour of other Men, without Envy, and without repining at our own Meanness, is a great Virtue; because these Things are not our Happiness, but for the Use and Convenience of this present Life; and to be contented with a little of them for present Use, is an Argument that we do not think them our Happiness, which is the true Excellency of this Virtue of Contentment: But to be contented, if we may so call it, to want that which is our true Happiness, or any Degree or Portion of it, to be contented never to enjoy the greatest and the best Things, is a Vice which contradicts the natural Desires of Happiness; and you may call it what you will, if you can think of any Name bad enough for it. It is the most despicable Temper in the World to have no Sense of true Honour or Happiness; or when we know there are greater and better Things, to take up with some low Enjoyments. And therefore, let the Thoughts of this ennoble our Minds, and since there are better Things in the other World, let us use our utmost Endeavours to possess ourselves of them, let us live like Men who are born for greater Things than this World affords; let us endeavour to inform ourselves, what the Happiness of the next World is, and how we may attain it: And let us use all present Things, as those who know there are infinitely greater and better Things reserv'd for us in the next World.

3. This should teach us also not to be over-concerned for the Shortness of our Lives. Our Lives indeed are very short, they fly away like a Shadow, and fade like the Flowers of the Field; and this were a very unsupportable Thought, were there either no Life after this, or not so happy a Life as this. But besides all the other Proofs we have of another Life, the very Shortness of our Lives may convince us, that Death does not put an End to our Being: For can we imagine, that so noble a Creature as Man is, was made for a Day! Man, I say, who is big with such immortal Designs, full of Projects for future Ages, who can look backward and forward and see an Eternity without Beginning, and without End: Who was made to contemplate

the

the Wonders of Nature and Providence, and to admire and adore his Maker; who is the Lord of this lower World; but has Eyes to look up to Heaven, and view all the Glories of it, and to pry into that invisible World, which this Veil of Flesh intercepts the Sight of. Man, who is so long a Child, and by such slow Steps arrives to the Use of Reason, and by that Time he has got a little Knowledge, and is earnestly seeking after more; by that Time he knows what it is to be a Man, and to what Purpose he ought to live; what God is, and how much he is bound to love and worship him; while he is ennobling his Soul with all heavenly Qualities and Virtues, and copying out the Divine Image; when the Glories of human Nature begin to appear, and to shine in him; that is, when he is most fit to live, to serve God and Men; then, I say, either this mortal Nature decays, and Dust returns to its Dust again, or some violent Distemper or evil Accident cuts him off in a vigorous Age; and when with great Labour and Industry he is become fit to live, he must live no longer. How is it possible to reconcile this with the Wisdom of God, if Man perishes when he dies; if he ceases to be as soon as he comes to be a Man? And therefore we have Reason to believe, that Death only translates us into another World, where the Beginnings of Wisdom and Virtue here, grow up into Perfection; and if that be a more happy Place than this World, as you have already heard, we have no Reason to quarrel that we live so little a while here: for setting aside the Miseries and Calamities, the Troubles and Inconveniencies of this Life, which the happiest Men are exposed to (for our Experience tells us, that there is no compleat and unmix'd Happiness here); setting aside, that this World is little else than a Scene of Misery to a great Part of Mankind, who struggle with Want and Poverty, labour under the Oppressions of Men, or the Pains and Sicknesses of diseased Bodies; yet if we were as happy as this World could make us, we should have no Reason to complain that we must exchange it for a much greater Happiness. We now call it Death, to leave this World; but were we once out of it, and instated in the Happiness of the next, we should think it were dying indeed to come into it again. We read of none of the Apostles, who did so passionately desire to be dissolved, and to be with Christ, as St *Paul*; and there was some Reason for it; because he had had a Taste of that Happiness, being snatched up into the third Heavens. Indeed, could we see the Glories of that Place, it would make us impatient of living here; and possibly that is one Reason why they are concealed from us; but yet Reason tells us, that if Death translates us to a better Place, the Shortness of our Lives here is an Advantage to us, if we take care to spend them well, for we shall be the sooner possess'd of a much happier Life.

III. From this Notion of Death, That it is our leaving this World, I observe farther what this Life is, only a State of Growth and Improvement, of Trial and Probation for the next. There can be no doubt of this, if we consider what the Scripture tells us of it, That we shall be rewarded in the next World, as we have behaved ourselves in this: That we shall receive according to what we have done in the Body, whether good or evil: Which proves, that this Life is only in order to the next; that our eternal Happiness or Misery shall bear Proportion to the Good or Evil which we have done here. And when we only consider, that after a short Continuance here, Man must be removed out of this World, if we believe that he does not utterly perish when he dies, but subsists still in another State, we have Reason to believe, that this Life is only a Preparation for the next: For why should a Man come into this World, and afterwards be removed into another, if this World had no Relation, nor Subordination to the next? Indeed, it is evident that Man is an improveable Creature, not created at first in the utmost Perfection of his Nature, nor put into the happiest State he is capable of, but trained up to Perfection and
Happiness

Happiness by Degrees. *Adam* himself in a State of Innocence, was but upon his good Behaviour, was but a Probationer for Immortality, which he forfeited for his Sin; and, as I observed before, it is most probable, that had he continued innocent, and refined and exalted his Nature by the Practice of divine Virtues, he would not have lived always in this World, but have been translated into Heaven. And I cannot see, how it is inconsistent with the Wisdom of God, to make some Creatures in a State of Probation; that as the angelical Nature was created so pure at first, as to be fit to live in Heaven; so Man, tho' an earthly, yet a reasonable, Creature, might be in a Capacity, by the Improvement of his natural Powers, of advancing himself thither. As it became the manifold Wisdom of God to create the Earth as well as the Heavens, so it became his Wisdom to make Man to inhabit this Earth; for it was not fitting that any Part of the World should be destitute of reasonable Beings, to know and adore their Maker, and to ascribe to him the Glory of his Works. But then, since a reasonable Nature is capable of greater Improvements than to live always in this World, it became the Divine Goodness to make this World only a State of Probation and Discipline for the next; that those who by a long and constant Practice of Virtue had spiritualized their Natures into a divine Purity, might ascend

ascend into Heaven, which is the true Center of all intelligent Beings. This seems to be the original Intention of God in making Man; and then this earthly Life was from the Beginning but a State of Growth and Improvement, to make us fit for Heaven, tho' without dying.

But to be sure the Scene is much altered now, for *Adam* by his Sin made himself mortal, and corrupted his own Nature, and propagated a mortal and corrupt Nature to his Posterity; and therefore we have no natural Right to Immortality, nor can we refine our Souls into such a divine Purity as is fit for Heaven, by the weaken'd and corrupted Power of Nature; but what we cannot do, Christ has done for us; he has purchased Immortality for us by his Death, and quickens and raises us into a new Life by his Spirit: But since still me must die, before we are immortal, it is more plain than ever, that this Life is only in order to the next, that the great Business, we have to do in this World, is to prepare ourselves for Immortality and Glory.

Now if our Life in this World be only in order to another Life, we ought not to expect our compleat Happiness here; for we are only in the Way to it; we must finish the Work God has given us to do in this World, and expect our Reward in the next; and if our Reward cannot be had in this World, we may conclude that there is something much better in the next World than any Thing here.

If

If this Life be our Time to work in, we should not consult our Ease and Softness, and Pleasures here; for this is a Place of Labour and Diligence, not of Rest: We are a travelling to Heaven, and must have our Eye on our Journey's End, and not hunt after Pleasures and Diversions in the Way.

The great End of living in this World, is to be happy in the next; and therefore we must wisely improve present Things, that they may turn to our future Account; must make to ourselves Friends of the Mammon of Unrighteousness, that when we fail, they may receive us into everlasting Habitations. What concerns a better Life, must take up most of our Thoughts and Care; and whatever endangers our future Happiness, must be rejected with all it's Charms. It would not be worth the while to live some few Years here, were we not to live for ever; and therefore it becomes a wise Man, who remembers that he must shortly leave this World, to make his present Life wholly subservient to his future Happiness.

SECT.

SECT. II.

The second Notion of Death, That it is our putting off these Bodies.

II. LET us now consider Death as it is our putting off these Bodies; for this is the proper Notion of Death, the Separation of Soul and Body, that the Body returns to Dust, the Soul or Spirit unto God who gave it. When we die, we do not cease to be, nor cease to live, but only cease to live in these earthly Bodies; the vital Union between Soul and Body is dissolved, we are no longer encloyster'd in a Tabernacle of Flesh, we no longer feel the Impressions of it, neither the Pains nor Pleasures of the Body can affect us, it can charm, it can tempt, no longer. This needs no Proof, but very well deserves our most serious Meditations.

For, 1. This teaches us the Difference and Distinction betwen Soul and Body, which Men who are sunk into Flesh and Sense, are apt to forget; nay, to lose the very Notion and Belief of it: All their Delights are fleshly, they know no other Pleasures but what their five Senses furnish them with; they cannot raise their Thoughts above this Body, nor entertain any noble Designs, and therefore they imagine, that they are nothing but Flesh and Blood, a little organized and animated

mated Clay; and it is no great Wonder, that Men who feel the Workings and Motions of no higher Principle of Life in them, but Flesh and Sense, should imagine that they are nothing but Flesh themselves. Though, methinks, when we see the senseless and putrifying Remains of a brave Man before us, it is hard to conceive that this is all of him; that this is the Thing which some few Hours ago could reason and discourse, was fit to govern a Kingdom, or to instruct Mankind, could despise Flesh and Sense, and govern all his bodily Appetites and Inclinations, and was adorned with all divine Graces and Virtues, was the Glory and Pride of the Age: And is this dead Carcase, which we now see, the Whole of him? Or was there a more divine Inhabitant, which animated this earthly Machine, which gave Life, and Beauty, and Motion to it, but is now removed?

To be sure, those who believe that Death does not put an End to their Being, but only removes them out of this Body, which rots in the Grave, while their Souls survive, live, and act, and may be happy in a separate State, should carefully consider this Distinction between Soul and Body, which would teach them a most divine and heavenly Wisdom.

For when we consider, That we consist of Soul and Body, which are the two distinct Parts of Man, this will teach us to take care of of both. For can any Man, who believes he has a Soul, be concerned only for his Body? A compound Creature cannot be happy, unless both Parts of him enjoy their proper Pleasures. He who enjoys only the Pleasures of the Body, is never the happier for having a human and reasonable Soul: The Soul of a Beast would have done as well, and it may be better; for brute Creatures relish bodily Pleasures as much, and it may be more, than Men do; and Reason is very troublesome to those Men who resolve to live like Brutes; for it makes them ashamed and afraid, which in many Cases hinders, or at least allays, their Pleasures. And why should not a Man desire the full and entire Happiness of a Man? Why should he despise any Part of himself, and that, as you shall hear presently, the best Part too? And therefore, at least, we ought to take as much care of our Souls as of our Bodies. Do we adorn our Bodies, that we may be fit to be seen, and to converse with Men, and may receive those Respects which are due to our Quality and Fortune; and shall we not adorn our Souls too with those Christian Graces, which make us lovely in the Sight of God and Men? The Ornament of a meek and quiet Spirit, which is in the Sight of God of great Price; which St *Peter* especially recommends to Christian Women, as a more valuable Ornament than the outward adorning of *plaiting the Hair*, or

wearing

wearing gold, or putting on apparel, 1 Pet. iii. 3, 4. The Ornaments of Wisdom and Prudence, of well-governed Passions, of Goodness and Charity, which give a Grace and Beauty to all our Actions, and such a pleasing and charming Air to our very Countenance, as the most natural Beauty, or artificial Washes and Paints can never imitate.

Are we careful to preserve our Bodies from any Hurt, from Pains and Sickness, from burning Fevers, or the racking Gout or Stone; and shall we not be as careful of the Ease of the Mind too? To quiet and calm those Passions, which when they grow outragious, are more intolerable than all natural or artificial Tortures? To moderate those Desires, which rage like Hunger and Thirst; those Fears which convulse the Mind with trembling and paralytick Motions; those furious Tempests of Anger, Revenge, and Envy, which ruffle our Minds, and fill us with Vexation, Restlessness, and Confusion of Thoughts; especially those guilty Reflections upon ourselves, that Worm in the Conscience which gnaws the Soul, and torments us with Shame and Remorse, and dreadful Expectations of an Avenger. These are the Sicknesses and Distempers of the Soul: These are Pains indeed, more sharp and pungent, and killing Pains than our Bodies are capable of: *The spirit of a man can bear his infirmity;* natural Courage, or the Powers of Reason, or the Comforts of Religion,

Religion, can support us under all other Sufferings? *but a wounded spirit who can bear?* and therefore a Man who loves Ease, should in the first place take care of the Ease of his Mind, for that will make all other Sufferings easy; but nothing can support a Man, whose Mind is wounded.

Are we fond of bodily Pleasures? Are we ready to purchase them at any Rate? And if we be Men, why would we despise the Pleasures of the Mind? If we have Souls, Why should we not reap the Benefit and the Pleasures of them? Do you think there are no Pleasures proper to the Soul? Have we Souls that are good for nothing? Or of no Use to us, but only to relish the Pleasures of the Body? Ask those who have tried, what the Pleasures of Wisdom and Knowledge are, which do as much excel the Pleasures of seeing, as Truth is more beautiful and glorious than the Sun: Ask them what a Pleasure it is to know God, the greatest and best Being, and the brightest Object of our Minds; to contemplate his Wisdom, and Goodness, and Power in the Works of Creation and Providence; to be swallowed up in that stupendious Mystery of Love, the Redemption of Sinners by the Incarnation and Sufferings of the Son of God? Ask them what the Pleasures of Innocence and Virtue are; what the Feast of a good Conscience means; which is the greatest Happiness, to give or to receive;

what the Joys even of Sufferings and Persecutions, of Want and Poverty, and Reproach are for the Sake of Chrift? Afk a devout Soul, What Tranfports and Ravifhment of Spirit he feels, when he is upon his Knees, when with St *Paul* he is even fnatched up into the Third Heavens, filled with God, overflowing with Praifes and Divine Joys? And does it not then become a Man, who has a reafonable Soul, to feek after thefe rational, thefe manly, thefe divine Pleafures, the Pleafures of the Mind and Spirit, which are proper and peculiar to a reafonable Creature? Let him do this, and then let him enjoy the Pleafures of the Body as much as he can, which will be very infipid and taftelefs, when his Soul is ravifhed with more noble Delights.

In a word, if we are fo careful to preferve the Life of our Bodies, which we know muft die, and rot and putrify in the Grave, methinks we fhould not be lefs careful to preferve the Life of our Souls, which is the only immortal Part of us. For though our Souls cannot die, as our Bodies do, yet they may be miferable, and that is called Eternal Death, where the Worm never dieth, and the Fire never goeth out. For to be always miferable, is infinitely worfe than not to be at all; and therefore is the moft formidable Death. And if we are fo unwilling to part with thefe mortal Bodies, we ought in Reafon son to be much more afraid to lose our Souls.

II. That Death is our putting off these Bodies, teaches us, that the Soul is the only Principle of Life and Sensation. The Body cannot live without the Soul, but as soon as it is parted from it, it loses all Sense and Motion, and returns to it's original Dust; but the Soul can and does live without the Body, and therefore there is the Principle of Life. This may be thought a very common and obvious Observation; and indeed so it is; but the Consequences of this are not so commonly observed, and yet are of great Use and Moment.

For, 1. This shews us, That the Soul is the best Part of us, that the Soul, indeed, is the Man, because it is the only Seat of Life and Knowledge, and all Sensations: For a Man is a living, reasonable, and understanding Being; and therefore a living, reasonable Soul (not an earthly Body, which has no Life or Sense, but what it derives from the Soul) must be the Man. Hence in Scripture Soul so frequently signifies the Man: Thus we read of the Souls that were born to *Jacob*, and the Souls that came with him into *Egypt*, Gen. xlvi. that is, his Sons. And Soul signifies ourselves; *a friend which is as thy own soul*; that is, as dear to us as ourselves, Deut. xiii. 6. And *Jonathan* loved *David* as *his own soul;* that is, as himself, 1 *Sam.* xviii. 3. For, in Propriety of Speech, the Body has no sense at all, but the Soul lives in the Body, and feels all the Motions and Impressions of it; so that it is the Soul only that is capable of Happiness or Misery, of Pain or Pleasure; and therefore it is the only Concernment of a wise Man to take care of his Soul; as our Saviour tells us, *What shall it profit a man, tho' he gain the whole world, and lose his own soul; or what shall a man give in exchange for his soul?* Matth. xvi. 26. The Reason of which is easily apprehended, when we remember, that the Soul only is capable of Happiness or Misery; that it is the Soul which must enjoy every thing else: And what can the whole World then signify to him who has no Soul to enjoy it, whose Soul is condemned to endless and eternal Miseries? Such a miserable Soul is as uncapable of enjoying the World, or any thing in it, as if it had lost it's Being.

2*dly,* Hence we learn the true Notion of bodily Pleasures, that they are such Pleasures as the Soul feels by it's Union to the Body; for it is not the Body that feels the Pleasures, but the Soul, though the Body be the Instrument of them. And therefore, how fond soever we are of them, we may certainly conclude, that bodily Pleasures are the meanest Pleasures of human Nature; because the Union to these earthly Bodies is the meanest

and

and most despicable State of reasonable Souls. These are not its proper and genuine Pleasures, which must result from its own Nature and Powers; but are only external Impressions, the light and superficial Touches of Matters; and it would be very absurd to conceive, that the Soul, which is the only Subject of Pleasure, should have no Pleasures of its own, but borrow its whole Happiness from its Affinity and Alliance to Matter; or that its greatest Pleasures should be owing to external Impressions, not to the Acting of its own natural Faculties and Powers: Which may convince us, as I observed before, that the Pleasures of the Mind are much the greatest and noblest Pleasures of the Man; and he who would be truly happy must seek for it, not in bodily Entertainments, but in the Improvements and Exercise of Reason and Religion.

3*dly*, Hence we learn also that the Body was made for the Soul, not the Soul for the Body; as that which in itself has no Life and Sense, is made for the Use of that which has. The Body is only a convenient Habitation for the Soul in this World, an Instrument of Action, and a Trial and Exercise of Virtue; but the Soul is to use the Body and to govern it, to taste its Pleasures, and to set Bounds to them, to make the Body serviceable to the Ends and Purposes of Reason and Virtue, not to subject Reason to Passion and Sense.

If the Body was made for the Use of the Soul, it was never intended the Soul should wholly conform itself to it, and by its Sympathy with corporeal Passions, transform itself into a sensual and brutish Nature. Such degenerate Creatures as those, who live only to serve the Body, who value nothing else, and seek for nothing else, but how to gratify their Appetites and Lusts: Which is to invert the Order of Nature, to fall in Love with their Slaves, and change Fortunes and Shackles with them. That our Saviour might well say, *He that committeth sin is the servant of sin:* For this is a vile and unnatural Subjection to serve the Body, which was made to serve the Soul; such Men shall receive the Reward of Slaves, to be turn'd out of God's Family, and not to inherit with Sons and Freemen; as our Saviour adds, *The servant abideth not in the house for ever, but the Son abideth for ever: If the Son therefore shall make you free, ye shall be free indeed,* John viii. 31, 32.

III. That Death, which is our leaving this World, is nothing else but our putting off these Bodies, teaches us, That it is only our Union to these Bodies, which intercepts the Sight of the other World. The other World is not at such a Distance from us as we may imagine: The Throne of God, indeed, is at a great Remove from this Earth, above the third

third Heavens, where he displays his Glory to those blessed Spirits which encompass his Throne; but as soon as we step out of these Bodies, we step into the other World, which is not so properly another World, (for there is the same Heaven and Earth still) as a new State of Life. To live in these Bodies, is to live in this World; to live out of them is to remove into the next. For while our Souls are confined to these Bodies, and can look only thro' these material Casements, nothing but what is material can affect us; nay, nothing but what is so gross, that can reflect Light, and convey the Shapes and Colours of Things with it to the Eye. So that though within this visible World there be a more glorious Scene of Things than what appears to us, we perceive nothing at all of it: For this Veil of Flesh parts the visible and invisible World. But when we put off these Bodies, there are new and surprising Wonders present themselves to our View; when these material Spectacles are taken off, the Soul with it's own naked Eyes sees what was invisible before: And then we are in the other World, when we can see it, and converse with it. Thus St *Paul* tells us, that *when we are at home in the body, we are absent from the Lord; but when we are absent from the body, we are present with the Lord,* 2 Cor. v. 6, 8. And methinks this is enough to cure us of our Fondness for these Bodies, unless we think it more desirable to be confined to a Prison, and to look through a Grate all our Lives, which gives us but a very narrow Prospect, and that none of the best neither, than to be set at Liberty to view all the Glories of the World. What would we give now for the least Glimpse of that invisible World, which the first Step we take out of these Bodies will present us with? There are such things *as Eye hath not seen, nor Ear heard, neither hath it entered into the Heart of man to conceive.* Death opens our Eyes, enlarges our Prospect, presents us with a new and more glorious World, which we can never see, while we are shut up in Flesh; which would make us as willing to part with this Veil, as to take the Film off of our Eyes which hinders our Sight.

IV. If we must put off these Bodies, methinks we should not much glory nor pride ourselves in them, nor spend too much of our Time about them. For why should that be our Pride, why should that be our Business, which we must shortly part with? And yet as for Pride, these mortal corruptible Bodies, and what relates to them, administer most of the Occasions of it.

Some Men glory in their Birth, and in their Descent from noble Ancestors, and ancient Families; which, besides the Vanity of it, for if we trace our Pedigree to their Original, it is certain, that all our Families are
equally

equally Ancient, and equally Noble; for we descend all from *Adam*; and in such a long Descent as this, no Man can tell, whether there have not been Beggars and Princes in those which are the noblest and ancientest Families now: Yet, I say, what is all this, but to pride ourselves in our Bodies, and our bodily Descent, unless Men think that their Souls are derived from their Parents too? Indeed our Birth is so very ignoble, whatever our Ancestors are, or however it may be dissembled with some pompous Circumstances, that no Man has any Reason to glory in it: For the greatest Prince is born like the wild Ass's Colt. Others glory in their external Beauty; which how great and charming soever it be, is but the Beauty of the Body, which if it be spared by Sickness and old Age, must perish in the Grave: Death will spoil those Features and Colours which are now admir'd; and, after a short time, there will be no Distinction between this beautiful Body, and common Dust. Others are guilty of greater Vanity than this, and what Nature has denied, they supply by Art; they adorn their Bodies with rich Attire, and many times such Bodies as will not be adorned; and then they glory in their borrowed Features: But what a sorry Beauty is that which they cannot carry into the other World? And if they must leave their Bodies in the Grave, I think there will be no great Occasion in the other

World,

World, for their rich and splendid Apparel, which will not fit a Soul.

Thus what do Riches signify, but to minister to the Wants and Conveniencies, and Pleasures of the Body? and therefore to pride ourselves in Riches, is to glory in the Body too; to think ourselves more considerable than other Men, because we can provide better for our Bodies than they can. And what a mean and contemptible Vice is Pride, whose Subject and Occasion is so mean and contemptible? To pride ourselves in these Bodies which have so ignoble an Extraction, are of so short a Continuance, and will have so ignoble an End, must lie down in the Grave, and be Food for Worms?

As for the Care of our Bodies; that must unavoidably take up great Part of our Time, to supply the Necessities of Nature, and to provide the Conveniencies of Life; but this may be for the Good of our Souls too, as honest Labour and Industry, and ingenious Arts are; but for Men to spend their whole Time in Sloth and Luxury, in Eating and Drinking, and Sleeping, in dressing, and adorning their Bodies, or gratifying their Lusts, this is to be vile Slaves and Servants to the Body, to Bodies which neither need nor deserve this from us: After all our Care they will tumble into Dust, and commonly much the sooner for our Indulgence of them.

V. If

V. If Death be our putting off these Bodies, then it is certain, that we must live without these Bodies 'till the Resurrection; nay, that we must always live without such Bodies as these are: For though our Bodies shall rise again, yet they shall be changed and transformed into a spiritual Nature; as St *Paul* expressly tells us, 1 *Cor.* xv. 42, 43, 44. *It is sown in corruption, it is raised in incorruption; it is sown in dishonour, it is raised in glory; it is sown in weakness, it is raised in power; it is sown a natural body, it is raised a spiritual body:* For, as he adds, *ver.* 50. *Flesh and blood cannot inherit the kingdom of God, neither can corruption inherit incorruption.* Which is true of a fleshly Soul; but here is understood of a Body of Flesh and Blood, which is of a corruptible Nature: As our Reason may satisfy us, that such gross earthly Bodies as we now carry about with us, cannot live and subsist in those pure Regions of Light and Glory which God inhabits; no more than you can lodge a Stone in the Air, or breathe nothing but pure Æther: And therefore our glorified Bodies will have none of these earthly Passions which these earthly Bodies have; will relish none of the Pleasures of Flesh and Blood; that upon this Account we may truly say, that when we once put off these Bodies, we shall ever after live without them.

Now

Now the Use of this Observation is so very obvious, that methinks no Man can miss it; for when we consider, that we must put off these Bodies, and for ever live without them, the very next Thought in Course is, that we ought to live without our Bodies now, as much as possibly we can, while we do live in them; to have but very little Commerce with Flesh and Sense; to wean ourselves from all bodily Pleasures; to stifle its Appetites and Inclinations, and to bring them under perfect Command and Government; that when we see it fit, we may use bodily Pleasures without Fondness, or let them alone without being uneasy for want of them; that is, that we may govern all our bodily Appetites, not they govern us.

For a wise Man should thus reason with himself: If I grow so fond of this Body, and the Pleasures of it: If I can relish no other Pleasures; If I value nothing else, What shall I do when I leave this Body? For bodily Pleasures can last no longer than my Body does: What shall I do in the next World, when I shall be stript of this Body, when I shall be a naked Soul? Or whatever other Covering I may have, shall have no Flesh and Blood about me; and therefore all the Pleasures I value now, will then vanish like a Dream; for it is impossible to enjoy bodily Pleasures when I have no Body. And though there were no other Punishments in the next Life,

Life, yet it is a great Pain to me now, to have my Defires difappointed or delayed; and fhould I retain the fame Fondnefs for thefe things in the next World, where they cannot be had, the eternal Defpair of enjoying them would be Punifhment enough.

Indeed we cannot tell what Alteration our putting off thefe Bodies will make in the Temper and Difpofition of our Minds. We fee that a long and fevere Fit of Sicknefs, while it lafts, will make Men abfolute Philofophers, and give them a great Contempt of bodily Pleafures; nay, will make the very Thoughts of thofe Pleafures naufeous, to them, which they were very fond of in Health. Long fafting and Abftinence, and other bodily Severities, are an excellent Means to alter the Habits and Inclinations of the Mind; and one would think, that to be feparated from thefe Bodies, muft needs make a greater Alteration in our Minds, than either Sicknefs or bodily Severities: That I dare not fay, That a fenfual Man, when he is feparated from this Body, fhall feel the fame fenfual Defires and Inclinations which he had in it, and fhall be tormented with a violent Thirft after thofe Pleafures which he cannot enjoy in a feparate State: But this I dare fay, That a Man who is wholly funk into Flefh and Senfe, and relifhes no other Pleafures, is not capable of living happily out of his Body; unlefs you could find out a new Scene

of

of material and sensible Pleasures to entertain him: For though the particular Appetites and Inclinations of the Body may cease, yet his very Soul is sensualized: And therefore is uncapable of the Pleasures of a spiritual Life.

For, indeed, setting aside that Mischief which the unruly Lusts and Appetites of Men and the immoderate Use of bodily Pleasures, does either to the Persons themselves, or to publick Societies; and the true Reason why we must mortify our sensual Inclinations, is to improve our Minds in all divine Graces: For the Flesh and the Spirit cannot thrive together; sensual and spiritual Joys are so contrary to each other, that which of them soever prevails, according to the Degrees of its Prevalence, it stifles and suppresses, or wholly subdues the other. A Soul which is ravished with the Love of God, and the blessed Jesus, transported with the spiritual Hopes of another Life, which feels the Passions of Devotion, and is enamour'd with the Glories and Beauties of Holiness and divine Virtues, must have such a very mean Opinion of Flesh and Sense, as will make it disgust bodily Pleasures, or be very indifferent about them: And a Soul which is under the Government of Sense and Passion, cannot taste those more intellectual and divine Joys; for it is our Esteem of Things which gives a Relish to them, and it is impossible we can highly esteem

esteem one, without depreciating and undervaluing the other: It is universally true in this Case, what our Saviour tells us, *No man can serve two masters: for either he will hate the one, and love the other; or else he will hold to the one, and despise the other: Ye cannot serve God and mammon*, Matth. vi. 24.

The least Beginnings of a divine Nature in us, is to love God above all the World; and as we every Day grow more devoutly and passionately in Love with God, and take greater Pleasure in the spiritual Acts of Religion, in praising God, and contemplating the Divine Nature and Perfections, and meditating on the spiritual Glories of another Life; so we abate of our Value for present Things, till we get a perfect Conquest and Mastery of them. But he who is perfectly devoted to the Pleasures of the Body, and Service of his Lusts, hath no spiritual Life in him; and though putting off these Bodies may cure our bodily Appetites and Passions; yet it cannot give us a new Principle of Life, nor work an essential Change in a fleshly Nature: And therefore such a Man, when he is removed from this Body, and all the Enjoyments of it, is capable of no other Happiness: Nay, though we are renewed by the Divine Spirit, and have a Principle of a new Life in us; yet, according to the Degree of our Love to present Things, so much the more indisposed are we for the Happiness of unbodied Spirits.

And

And therefore, since we must put off these Bodies, if we would live for ever happily without them, we must begin betimes to shake off Matter and Sense, to govern our bodily Appetites and Passions; to grow indifferent to the Pleasures of Sense, to use them for the Refreshment and Necessities of Nature, but not to be over-curious about them, not to be fond of enjoying them, nor troubled for the Want of them; never to indulge ourselves in unlawful Pleasures, and to be very temperate in our Use of lawful ones; to be sure we must take care that the spiritual Part, that the Sense of God, and of Religion, be always predominant in us; and this will be a Principal of Life in us, a Principle of divine Sensations and Joys, when this Body shall tumble into Dust.

VI. If Death be our putting off these Bodies, then the Resurrection from the Dead is the Re-union of Soul and Body. The Soul does not die, and therefore cannot be said to rise again from the Dead; but it the Body, which like Seed falls into the Earth, and springs up again more beautiful and glorious at the Resurrection of the Just. To believe the Resurrection of the Body, or of the Flesh; and to believe another Life after this, are two very different Things: The Heathens believed a future State, but never dream'd of the Resurrection of the Body, which is the

peculiar

peculiar Article of the Christian Faith. And yet it is the Resurrection of our Bodies, which is our Victory and Triumph over Death; for Death was the Punishment of *Adam*'s Sin, and those who are in a separate State, still suffer the Curse of the Law, *Dust thou art, and to dust thou shalt return*. Christ came to deliver us from this Curse, by being made a Curse for us; that is, to deliver us from Death by dying for us. But no Man can be said to be delivered from Death, 'till his Body rise again; for Part of him is under the Power of Death still, while his Body rots in the Grave: Nay, he is properly in a State of Death, while he is in a State of Separation of Soul and Body, which is the true Notion of Death. And therefore St *Paul* calls the Resurrection of the Body, the destroying Death, 1 *Cor.* xv. 25, 26. *He must reign 'till he hath put all enemies under his feet; the last enemy that shall be destroyed is death:* That is, by the Resurrection of the Dead, as appears from the whole Scope of the Place, and is particularly expressed, *ver.* 54, 55, &c. *So when this corruptible shall have put on incorruption, and this mortal shall have put on immortality, then shall be brought to pass that saying, which is written, Death is swallowed up in Victory: O death where is thy sting! O grave where is thy victory! The sting of death is sin, and the strength of sin is the law; but blessed be God, who hath given us the victory, through our Lord Jesus Christ,*

Chrift. This is the Perfection and Confummation of our Reward, when our Bodies fhall be raifed Incorruptible and glorious; when Chrift fhall change our vile Bodies, and make them like to his own moft glorious Body. I doubt not but good Men are in a very happy State before the Refurrection, but yet their Happinefs is not compleat; for the very State of Separation is an imperfect State, becaufe a feparate Soul is not a perfect Man: A Man, by the original Conftitution of his Nature, confifts of a Soul and Body; and therefore his perfect Happinefs requires the united Glory and Happinefs of both Parts, of the whole Man. Which is not confidered by thofe who cannot apprehend any Neceffity why the Body fhould rife again; fince, as they conceive, the Soul might be as compleatly and perfectly happy without it. But yet the Soul would not be an entire and perfect Man; for a Man confifts of Soul and Body: A Soul in a State of Separation, how happy foever otherwife it may be, has ftill this Mark of God's Difpleafure on it, that it has loft it's Body; and therefore the Re-union of our Souls and Bodies has at leaft this Advantage in it, that it is a perfect Reftoring of us to the divine Favour; that the Badge and Memorial of our Sin and Apoftacy is done away, in the Refurrection of our Bodies; and therefore this is called *the Adoption,* viz. *the Redemption of our Body,* Rom. viii. 23. For then it

is

is that God publickly owns us for his Sons, when he raises our dead Bodies into a glorious and immortal Life. And besides this, I think we have no Reason to doubt but the Re-union of Soul and Body will be a new Addition of Happiness and Glory; for tho' we cannot guess what the Pleasures of glorified Bodies are; yet sure we cannot imagine, that when these earthly Bodies are the Instruments of so many Pleasures, a spiritual and glorified Body should be of no Use: A Soul and Body cannot be vitally united, but there must be a Sympathy between them, and receive mutual Impressions from each other; and then we need not doubt, but that such glorified Bodies will highly minister, though in a way unknown to us, to the Pleasures of a divine and perfect Soul; will infinitely more contribute to the divine Pleasures of the Mind, than these earthly Bodies do to our sensual Pleasures. That all who have this Hope and Expectation may, as St *Paul* speaks, *Earnestly groan within themselves, waiting for the adoption, even the redemption of our bodies*, Rom. viii. 23. This being the Day of the Marriage of the Lamb, this consummates our Happiness; when our Bodies and Souls meet again, not to disturb and oppose each other, as they do in this World, where the Flesh and the Spirit are at perpetual Enmity; but to live in eternal Harmony, and to heighten and inflame each others Joys.

Now this Confideration, that Death being a putting off thefe Bodies the Refurrection of the Dead muft be a raifing of our Bodies into a new and immortal Life, and the Re-union of them to our Souls, fuggefts many ufeful Thoughts to us: For

This teaches us how we are to ufe our Bodies, how we are to prepare them for Immortality and Glory. Death, which is the Separation of Soul and Body, is the Punifhment of Sin, and indeed it is the Cure of it too; for Sin is fuch a Leprofy as cannot be perfectly cleanfed without pulling down the Houfe, which it has once infected: But if we would have thefe Bodies raifed up again immortal and glorious, we muft begin the Cleanfing and Purification of them here. We muft be *fanctified throughout, both in body, foul, and spirit*, 1 Theff. v. 23. Our Bodies muft be the Temples of the Holy Ghoft, muft be holy and confecrated Places, 1 *Cor*. vi. 7. Muft not be polluted with filthy Lufts, if we would have them rebuilt again by the Divine Spirit, after the Defolations which Sin hath made. Thus St *Paul* tells us at large, *Rom*. viii. 10, 11, 12, 13. *And if Chrift be in you, the body is dead, becaufe of fin; but the fpirit is life, becaufe of righteoufnefs*: That is, that divine and holy Nature, which we receive from Chrift, will fecure the Life of our Souls, and tranflate us to a happy State after Death; but it will not fecure us from the Neceffity

of

of dying: Our Bodies must die as a Punishment of Sin, and putrify in the Grave; but yet they are not lost for ever: *For if the spirit of him that raised up Jesus from the dead, dwell in you; he that raised up Christ from the dead, shall quicken your mortal bodies by his spirit which dwelleth in you*; that is, if your Bodies be cleansed and sanctified, be the Temples of the Holy Spirit, he will raise them, up again into a new Life: *Therefore, brethren, we are debtors, not to the flesh, to live after the flesh; for if ye live after the flesh, ye shall die; but if ye through the spirit do mortify the deeds of the body, ye shall live:* If ye subdue the fleshly Principle, if ye bring the Flesh into Subjection to the Spirit, not only your Souls shall live, but your Bodies shall be raised again to immortal Life. And this is a mighty Obligation to us, if we love our Bodies and would have them glorious and immortal, not to pamper the Flesh, and gratify it's Appetites and Lusts; *not to yield your members servants to uncleanness, and to iniquity unto iniquity; but to yield your members servants to righteousness unto holiness; that being made free from sin, and becoming the servants of God, you may have your fruit unto holiness, and the end everlasting life,* as the same Apostle speaks, Rom. vii. 19, 22. It is our Relation to Christ, that our very Bodies are his Members; it is our Relation to the Holy Spirit that our Bodies are his Temples, which entitles our

Death; what we call a natural Death is very inglorious, it is a Mark of Dishonour, because it is a Punishment Sin: Such Bodies at best are sown in Dishonour and Corruption, as St *Paul* speaks; but to die a Martyr, to fall a Sacrifice to God, this is a glorious Death; this is not to yield to the Laws of Mortality, to Necessity and Fate, but to give back our Bodies to God, who gave them us; and he will keep that which we have committed to his Trust, to a glorious Resurrection; and it will be a surprising and astonishing Glory with which such Bodies shall rise again, as have suffered for their Lord; *for if we suffer with him we shall also be glorified together:* Which seems to imply, that those shall nearest resemble the Glory of Christ himself who suffer as he did.

This is the Way to make our Bodies immortal and glorious. We cannot keep them long here, they are corruptible Bodies, and will tumble into Dust; we must part with them for a while, and if ever we expect and desire a happy Meeting again, we must use them with Modesty and Reverence now. We dishonour our Bodies in this World, when we make them Instruments of Wickedness and Lust, lay an eternal Foundation of Shame and Infamy for them in the next World; it is a mortal and killing Love, to cherish the fleshly Principle, to make Provision for the Flesh to fulfil the Lusts thereof: But if you love

love your Bodies, make them immortal, that though they die, they may rise again out of their Graves with a youthful Vigour and Beauty; that they may live for ever without Pain and Sickness, without the Decays of Age, or the Interruptions of Sleep, or the Fatigue or Weariness of Labour; without wanting either Food or Raiment, without the least Remains of Corruption, without knowing what it is to tempt, or to be tempted, without the least uneasy Thought, the least Disappointment, the least Care, in the full and blissful Enjoyment of the Eternal and Sovereign Good.

SECT. III.

Death consider'd as our Entrance upon a new and unknown State of Life.

III. LET us now consider Death as it is an Entrance upon a new and unknown State of Life; for it is a new Thing to us to live without these Bodies, it is what we have never tried yet, and we cannot guess how we shall feel ourselves, when we are stript of Flesh and Blood; what Entertainments we shall find in that Place, where there is neither eating nor drinking, neither marrying, nor giving in Marriage; what kind of Business and Employment we shall have there, where we shall have no Occasion for any of these our Time here; ... Food, or Raiment, ... dwell in, or ... Bodies make necessary ... Trades and Arts, ... Conveniences for ... This ... needs be a very ... though we are ... in the next World, ... whatever ... Pleasure here; yet most ... change a known ... confounds ... going out of ... Body ... whither. Now ... suggest several very ...

... Trust and Faith in God. ... without it ... World ... we cannot die ... without ... this is the noblest Exercise of Faith, to be chearfully to resign up our Selves into the Hands of God, when we know so little of the State of the other World whither we are going. This was the first Tral of *Abraham's* Faith, when, in Obedience to the Command of God, he forsook his own Country, and his Father's House, and followed God into a strange Land, Heb. xi. 1. *By faith Abraham, when he was called to go into a place, which he should after receive for an inheritance, obeyed; and he went out,*

out, not knowing whither he went. Canaan was the Type of Heaven; and Heaven is as unknown a Country to us, as *Canaan* was to *Abraham*. And herein we must imitate this Father of the Faithful, to be contented to leave our Native Country, and the World we know, to follow God whithersoever he leads us, into unknown Regions, and to an unknown and unexperienced Happiness. This indeed all Men must do, because they cannot avoid leaving this World, but must go when God calls for them: But that which makes it our Choice, an Act of Faith and Virtue, is this, such a strong Persuasion, and firm Reliance on the Goodness, and Wisdom, and Promises of God, that though we are ignorant of the State of the other World, we can chearfully forsake all our known Enjoyments, and embrace the Promises of an unknown Happiness. And there are two distinct Acts of this, which answer to *Abraham's* Faith in leaving his own Country, and following God into a strange Land: The first is the Exercise of our Faith while we live; the second when we die.

To mortify all our inordinate Appetites and Desires, to deny ourselves the sinful Vanities and Pleasures of this Life, for the Promises of an unknown Happiness in the next, is our mystical dying to this World, leaving our native Country, and following God into a strange and unknown Land; to quit all our
present

present Possessions in this World, to forfeit our Estates or Liberties, all that is dear to us here; nay, to forsake our native Country, rather than to offend God, and lose our Title to the Promises of an unknown Happiness, is, in a literal Sense, to leave our own Country at God's Command, not knowing whither we go; which is like *Abraham*'s going out of his own Country, and living as a Sojourner in the Land of Promise, without having an Inheritance in it. This is that Faith which overcomes the World, which makes us live as Pilgrims and Strangers here, as those who seek for another Country, for a heavenly *Canaan*, as the Apostle tells us *Abraham* did: *For by faith he sojourned in the land of promise, as in a strange country, dwelling in tabernacles with Isaac and Jacob, the heirs with him of the same promise; for he looked for a city which has foundations, whose builder and maker is God,* Heb. xi. 9, 10.

And when we come to die, and can with Joy and Triumph, in an Assurance of God's Promises, commend our Spirits to him, and trust him with our Souls, when we know not the Country we go to, and never experienced what the Happiness of it is, without any Concern or Sollicitude about it; this is a noble Act of Faith, which does great Honour to God, and conquers all the natural Aversions to Death, and makes it an easy Thing to leave this World, and the Object of our De-
fire

fire and Choice, to see that promised Land, and taste those Pleasures which we are yet Strangers to. We must live, and we must die in Faith too, as the Patriarchs did, who all died in Faith, not having received the Promises, but seeing them afar off. And for that Reason, the other World must be in a great measure unknown to us; for could we see it, could we before-hand taste the Pleasures of it, or know what they are, it would be no Act of Faith to leave this World for it, to be willing to be translated from Earth to Heaven: But no Man is worthy of Heaven, who dares not take God's Word for it; and therefore God has concealed those Glories from us, and given us only a Promise of a great, but an unknown Happiness, for the Object of our Hope, to be a Trial of our Faith, and Obedience, and Trust, in him.

That the other World is an unknown State to us, trains us up to a great Trust and Confidence in God: For we must trust God for our Souls, and for the next World; and this naturally teaches us to trust God in this World too, to live securely upon his Providence, and to suffer him to dispose of us as he pleases.

Indeed, no Man can trust God in this World, who has not a stedfast Faith in God, for the Rewards of the next. For the external Administrations of Providence are not always what we could wish; but good Men are very well contented, and have great Reason to be so, to take this World and the next together; and therefore are not sollicitous about present Things, but leave God to chuse what Condition for them he pleases, as being well assured of his Goodness, who has prepared for them eternal Rewards.

And those who can trust God with their Souls, who can trust him for an immortal Life, for an unseen and unknown Happiness, will find no Difficulty in trusting him for this World; I mean those who are concern'd for their future Happiness, and take any care of their Souls. If all who are unconcern'd for their Souls, and never trouble their Heads what will become of them hereafter, may be said to trust God with their Souls, then, I confess this will not hold true; for the greatest Number of those who thus trust God with their Souls will trust him for nothing else. But this is not to trust God, but to be careless of our Souls. But now, when a Man who stedfastly believes another Life after this, and is heartily concerned what will become of him for ever, can securely rely on God's Promises, beyond his own Knowledge and Prospect of Things; he will very easily trust God for every Thing else: For he is not so sollicitous about any thing in this World, as he is for his Soul; and if he can trust God with his dearest Interests, surely he will trust him in less Matters. The Promises of eternal

nal Life, through our Lord Jesus Christ, are the highest Demonstration of God's Love to us; and he who is so well assured of God's Love, that he can trust him for Heaven, can never distrust his Care and Providence in this World. The Methods of God's Providence can never be so unknwn to us in this World, as the State of the other World is unknown: And if we can chearfully follow God into an unseen and unknown World, cannot we be contented to follow him through the most dark and perplexed Tracks of Providence here? so that we have as little Reason to complain, that the State of the other World is unknown to us, as we have, that we must live by Faith in this World; for absent, unseen, and unknown Things, are the Objects of our Faith. And those who will trust God no farther than they can see, neither in this World, nor in the next, have no Reason to depend upon his Providence here, nor to expect Heaven hereafter.

2*dly*, The State of the other World being so much unknown to us, is a very good Reason why we should chearfully comply with all the Terms and Conditions of the Gospel; to do whatever our Saviour requires, that we may obtain eternal Life. This, it may be, you will not so readily apprehend, and yet the Reason of it is very plain; for since the State of the other World is so much unknown to us, we do not, and cannot know neither, what

what Difpofitions, and Habits, and Complexion of Soul are neceffary to fit and qualify us for this unknown Happinefs. But our Saviour, who knew what that State is, knew alfo what is neceffary to that State; and therefore the wifeft Courfe we can take, is to obey all his Laws without any Difpute, not only as the Conditions of Happinefs, without which we fhall not be admitted into Heaven, but as the neceffary Preparations for it. As to explain this by a parallel Cafe, which you will eafily underftand: Suppofe we had pre-exifted in a former State, as fome fay we did, before we came into thefe Bodies: And before we knew any thing of this World, or what the Pleafure and Entertainments of it are, fhould have been told what kind of Bodies we muft go into, no doubt but there would have been wonderful wife Difputes about the Make and Frame of our Bodies; we fhould have thought fome Parts fuperfluous or ufelefs, or ill contrived; indeed, fhould have wonder'd, what fuch a Body was made for, as well we might, before we underftood the Ufe of any Part of it; but God who knew what he intended us for, provided fuch a Body for us, as is both beautiful and ufeful; and we cannot want any Part of it, but we are depriv'd of fome Conveniencies and Pleafures of Life. And thus we may eafily fuppofe it to be with reference to the next World; that the Habits and Tempers of our Minds

are

are as neceſſary to reliſh the Pleaſures of that State, as our bodily Senſes are to taſte bodily Pleaſures; and ſince we do not particularly know what the Delights of that State are, and Chriſt does, we ought as perfectly to reſign up ourſelves to his Directions for the faſhioning our Minds, as we truſt God to form our Bodies for us. Whatever Graces and Virtues he requires us to exerciſe in this World, though we do not ſee the preſent Uſe of them, though we may think them an unneceſſary Reſtraint of our Liberties, and very needleſs and unreaſonable Severities; yet we ought to conclude, that Chriſt knew the Reaſon of ſuch Commands, and that ſuch Qualities and Diſpoſitions of Mind will be found as neceſſary in the next World, as our bodily Senſes are here.

And this we ought eſpecially to conclude of ſuch Degrees and Inſtances of Virtue, as ſeem above our preſent State, and not ſo well fitted to our Condition of Life in this World: For why ſhould our Saviour give us ſuch Laws, and exact ſuch a Degree of Virtue from us, here, as abridges our preſent Enjoyments, and (it may be) expoſe us to great Inconveniencies and Sufferings, were not that Temper of Mind which theſe Virtues form in us, of great Uſe and Neceſſity in the next Life? As for Inſtance:

We ſhould think it ſufficient, while we live in this World, where there are ſo many inviting Objects, and while we are cloathed with Bodies of Flesh, which are made for the Enjoyments of Sense, and have natural Appetites and Inclinations to them, so to govern ourselves in the Use of these Pleasures, as neither to make ourselves Beasts, nor to injure our Neighours; and while we keep within these Bounds, to gratify our Appetites and Inclinations to the full. For it is certainly the Happiness of an earthly Creature to enjoy this World, though a reasonable Creature must do it reasonably. *But not to love this World*, it seems a hard Command to a Creature who lives in it, and was made to enjoy it. To despise bodily Pleasures, to subdue the fleshly Principle in us, not only to Reason, but to the Spirit; to live above the Body, and to strive to stifle not only its irregular, but even its natural Appetite; and to taste the Pleasures of it very sparingly, and with great Indifference of Mind, seems a very hard Saying to Flesh and Blood. We should think it Time enough to have our Conversation in Heaven, when we come thither; but it is plainly above the State of an earthly Creature to live in Heaven, to have all our Joys, our Hopes, our Treasure, and our Hearts there. The State of this World would be very happy and prosperous without such a raised, and refined, and spiritualized Mind, and therefore these are such Virtues as are not necessary to the present Constitution of this World,

World, and therefore can be only in order to the next.

Thus, it is sufficient to the Happiness and good Government of this World, that Men do no Injury to each other, and that they express mutual Civilities and Respects; that they take care of those whom Nature has endeared to them; and that they be just, and in ordinary Cases helpful to others; and therefore this is all that the State of this World requires. But that divine and universal Charity, which teaches us to love all Men as ourselves, even our Enemies, and those who hate and persecute us; to forgive the Injuries we suffer, and not to revenge and retaliate them, not to render Evil for Evil, nor Railing for Railing, but contrariwise, Blessing: I say, this wonderful Virtue does not only lie extremely cross to Self-love, but it is hardly reconcileable with the State of this World. For the Practice of it is very dangerous, when we live among bad Men; who will take Advantage of such a bearing and forgiving Virtue, to give great Occasions for the constant Exercise of it; and nothing but a particular Providence, which watches over such good Men, can secure them from being an easy Prey to the Wicked and unjust. Nay, we see, this is not practicable in the Government of the World: Civil Magistrates are forced to punish Evil-doers, or the World would be a *Bedlam*; and therefore those who have thought such publick Executions of Juſtice to be inconſiſtent with this Law of forgiving Injuries, and not revenging ourſelves, have made it unlawful for Chriſtians to be Magiſtrates, becauſe hanging or whipping, or pillorying Malefactors, is not forgiving them, as certainly it is not. A very abſurd Doctrine, which makes it neceſſary that there ſhould always be Heathens in every Nation, to govern even a Chriſtian Kingdom, or that the Chriſtian World ſhould have no Government at all, tho' nominal and profeſs'd Chriſtians have as much need of Government, as ever any Heathens had. But this forgiving Enemies is only a private Virtue, not the Rule of Publick Government; which ſhews, that the State of this World is ſo far from requiring this Virtue, that it will admit only the private Exerciſe of it, and that too under the Protection of a particular Providence to defend thoſe good Men who muſt not avenge themſelves. Now ſuch Virtues as the State of this World does not require, we muſt conclude, are only in order to the next; and that though we do not ſo well diſcern the Reaſon and Uſe of this divine Charity here, yet this Temper of Mind is abſolutely neceſſary to the Happineſs of the other World; and for that Reaſon it is, that Chriſt requires the Exerciſe of it now: For we cannot imagine any other Reaſon why our Saviour ſhould make any Acts of Virtue, which the State of this World does not re-

quire

quire the present Exercise of, the necessary Terms and Conditions of our future Happiness, but only that such Dispositions of Mind are as necessary to qualify us to relish those divine Pleasures, as our Bodily Senses are to perceive the Delights and Pleasures of this World. This is a mighty Obligation on us to obey the Laws of our Saviour, as the Methods of our Advancement to eternal Glory; not to dispute his Commands, how uneasy or unreasonable soever they may now appear; for the Reasons of them are not to be fetched from this World, but from the next; and therefore are such, as we cannot so well understand now, because we know so little of the next World; but we may safely conclude, that Christ knows a Reason for it, and that we shall quickly understand the Reason of it, when we come into the other World: And therefore we should endeavour to exercise all those Heights of Virtue, which the Gospel recommends to us; for as much as we fall short of these, so will our Glory and Happiness abate in the other World.

3*dly*, Tho' the State we enter on at Death be in a great Measure unknown to us; yet this no reasonable Discouragement to good Men, nor Encouragement to the bad. 1. It is no reasonable Discouragement to good Men; for though we do not know what it is, yet we know it is a great Happiness: So it is represented to us in Scripture, as a Kingdom, and a Crown, an eternal Kingdom, and a never-fading Crown. Now would any Man be unwilling to leave a mean and homely Cottage, to go and take Poſſeſſion of a Kingdom, becauſe he had never yet ſeen it, though he had heard very glorious Things of it from very faithful and credible Witneſſes? For let us a little conſider in what Senſe the Happineſs of the other World is unknown.

1. That it is not ſuch a kind of Happineſs as is in this World, that it is like nothing that we have ſeen or taſted yet: But a wiſe and good Man cannot think this any Diſparagement to the other World, though it would have been a real Diſparagement to it, had it been like this World: For here is nothing but Vanity and Vexation of Spirit, nothing but an empty Scene, which makes a fine Show, but has no real and ſolid Joys. Good Men have enough of this World, and are ſufficiently ſatisfied that none of theſe Things can make them happy, and therefore cannot think it any Diſadvantage to change the Scene, and try ſome unknown and unexperienced Joys: For if there be ſuch a Thing as Happineſs to be found, it muſt be ſomething which they have not known yet, ſomething that this World does not afford.

2. When we ſay that the State of the other World is unknown, the only Meaning of it is, That it is a State of ſuch Happineſs, ſo far beyond any Thing we ever experienced yet;

that

that we cannot form any Notion or Idea of it: We know that there is such a Happiness; we know in some measure wherein this Happiness consists; *viz.* in seeing God, and the blessed Jesus, who loved us, and gave himself for us; in praising our great Creator and Redeemer; in conversing with Saints and Angels. But how great, how ravishing and transporting a Pleasure this is, we cannot tell, because we never yet felt it: Our dull Devotions, our imperfect Conceptions of God in this World, cannot help us to guess what the Joys of Heaven are; we know not how the Sight of God, how the Thoughts of him, will pierce our Souls; with what Extasies and Raptures we shall sing the Song of the Lamb; with what melting Affections perfect Souls shall embrace; what Glories and Wonders we shall there see and know; *Such things as neither eye hath seen, nor ear heard, neither hath it entered into the heart of Man to conceive.* Now methinks this should not make the Thoughts of Death uneasy to us, should not make us unwilling to go to Heaven, that the Happiness of Heaven is too great for us to know or to conceive in this World. For,

3. Men are naturally fond of unknown and untried Pleasures; which is so far from being a Disparagement to them, that it raises our Expectations of them, that they are unknown. In the Things of this World, Enjoyment usually lessens our Esteem and Value

for them, and we always value that moſt which we have never tried; and methinks the Happineſs of the other World ſhould not be the only Thing we deſpiſe, before we try it. All preſent Things are mean, and appear to be ſo when they are enjoyed: But whatever Expectations we have of the unknown Happineſs of the other World, the Enjoyment of it will as much exceed our biggeſt Expectations as other Things uſually fall below them; that we ſhould be forced to confeſs with the Queen of *Sheba*, when we ſaw *Solomon*'s Glory, that not the half of it was told her.

It is ſome Encouragement to us, that the Happineſs of Heaven is too big to be known in this World; for did we perfectly know it now, it could not be very great; and therefore we ſhould entertain ourſelves with the Hopes of this unknown Happineſs, of thoſe Joys which we now have ſuch imperfect Conceptions of. 2. Nor is it, on the other hand, any Encouragement to bad Men, that the Miſeries of the other World are unknown: For it is known that God has threatned very terrible Puniſhments, againſt bad Men; and that what theſe Puniſhments are, is unknown, makes them a great deal more formidable. For who knows the Power of God's Wrath? Who knows how miſerable God can make bad Men? This makes it a ſenſeleſs Thing for Men to harden themſelves againſt the Fears of the other World, becauſe they know not

what

what it is; and how then can they tell, tho' they could bear up under all known Miseries, but that there may be such Punishments as they cannot bear? That they are unknown, argues that they are something more terrible than they are acquainted with in this World. They are represented indeed by the most dreadful and terrible Things; by Lakes of Fire and Brimstone, Blackness and Darkness, the Worm that never dieth, and the Fire that never goeth out. But bad Men think this cannot be true in a literal Sense; that there can be no Fire to burn Souls, and torment them eternally. Now suppose it were so; yet if they believe these Threatnings, they must believe that some terrible Thing is signified by everlasting Burnings; and if Fire and Brimstone serve only for Metaphors to describe those Torments by, what will the real Sufferings of the Damned be! For the Spirit of God does not use to describe Things by such Metaphors as are greater than the Things themselves. And therefore let no bad Man encourage himself in Sin, because he does not know what the Punishments of another World are. This should possess us with the greater Awe and Dread of them, since every thing in the other World, not only the Happiness, but the Miseries of it, will prove greater, not less than we expect.

CHAP.

CHAP. II.

Concerning the Certainty of our Death.

HAving thus shewed you under what Notions we are to consider Death, and what Wisdom we should learn from them, I proceed to the Second Thing, the Certainty of Death: *It is appointed unto men once to die:* ἀπόκειται it remains, it is reserved, and as it were laid up for them.

I believe no Man will desire a Proof of this, which he sees with his Eyes; one Generation succeds another, and those who live longest, at last yield to the fatal Stroke. There were two Men indeed, *Enoch* and *Elias*, who did not die, as Death signifies a Separation of Soul and Body, but were translated to Heaven without dying; but this is the general Law for Mankind, from which none are excepted, but those whom God by his sovereign Authority, and for wise Reasons, thinks fit to except; which have been but two since the Creation, and will be no more 'till Christ comes to judge the World: For then St *Paul* tells us, those who are alive at Christ's second coming, shall not die, but shall be changed, 1 Cor. xv. 51, 52. *Behold, I shew you a mystery; we shall not all sleep,*
but

but we shall all be changed in a moment, in the twinkling of an eye, at the last trump; for the trumpet shall sound, and the dead shall be raised incorruptible, and we shall be changed. This is such a Change as is equivalent to Death, it puts us in the same State with those who are dead, and at the last Judgment rise again.

SECT. I.

A Vindication of the Justice and Goodness of GOD, in appointing Death for all Men.

BUT before I shew you what Use to make of this Consideration, That we must all certainly die; let us examine how Mankind comes to be mortal: This was no Dispute among the Heathens, for it was no great Wonder that an earthly Body should die, and dissolve again into Dust: It would be a much greater Wonder to see a Body of Flesh and Blood preserved in perpetual Youth and Vigour, without any Decays of Nature, without being sick or growing old. But this is a Question among us; or if it may not be called a Question, yet it is what deserves our Consideration, since we learn from the History of *Moses*, that as frail and brittle as these earthly Tabernacles are, yet if Man had not sinned, he had not died.

When

When God created Man, and placed him in Paradise, he forbad him to eat of the Tree of Knowledge, of Good and Evil: *Of every tree of the garden thou may'st freely eat, but of the tree of the knowledge of good and evil thou shalt not eat of it; for in the day thou eatest thereof, thou shalt surely die,* Gen. ii. 16, 17. And when, notwithstanding this Threatning, our first Parents did eat of it, GOD confirms and ratifies the Sentence, *Dust thou art, and to dust thou shalt return,* Gen. iii. 19. What this Tree of Knowledge of Good and Evil was, is as great a Mystery to us, as what the Tree of Life was; for we understand neither of them; which makes some Men, who would not be thought to be ignorant of any thing, to fly to allegorical Senses: But tho' I would be glad to know this, if I could, yet I must be contented to leave it a Mystery, as I find it. That which we are concerned in is, That this Sentence of Death and Mortality, which was pronounced on *Adam,* fell on all his Posterity: As St *Paul* tells us, 1 Cor. xv. 21, 22. *That by man came death; and in Adam all die.* And this he does not only assert but prove, *Rom.* v. 12, 13, 14. *Wherefore by man sin entered into the world, and death by sin, and so death passed upon all men, for that all have sinned: For until the law, sin was in the world; but sin is not imputed where there is no law; nevertheless death reigned from Adam 'till Moses, even over them who had not sinned after the similitude of Adam's transgression*. The Design of all which is to prove, that Men die, or are mortal, not for their own Sins, but for the Sin of *Adam*: Which the Apostle proves by this Argument; because though all Men, as well as *Adam*, have sinned, yet 'till the giving the Law of *Moses*, there was no Law which threatened Death against Sin, but only that Law given to *Adam* in Paradise, which no Man else ever did, or ever could transgress, but he. Now *sin is not imputed where there is no law*: That is, it is not imputed to any Man to Death, before there is any Law, which threatens Death against it: That no Man can be reckoned to die for those Things, which no Law punishes with Death. Upon what Account then, says the Apostle, could those Men die, who lived between *Adam* and *Moses*, before the Law was given, which threatens Death? And yet die they all did, even those *who had not sinned after the similitude of Adam's transgression*; who had neither eaten the forbidden Fruit, nor sinned against any other express Law threatening Death: This could be for no other Sin but *Adam*'s; he sinned, and brought Death into the World, and thus Death passed upon all Men for his Sin, notwithstanding they themselves were Sinners; for though they were Sinners, yet that they died was not owing to their own Sins, because they had not sinned against any Law which threatened Death, but to the Sin

of

of *Adam*; and therefore in a proper Senſe, *in Adam all die.*

Now this is thought very hard, that the Sin of *Adam* ſhould bring Death upon all his Poſterity; that one Man ſinned, and all Men muſt die; and therefore, I ſuppoſe, no Man will think it improper to my preſent Argument, to give you ſuch an Account of this Matter, as will evidently juſtify the Wiſdom and Goodneſs, as well as the Juſtice, of GOD in it.

I. In the firſt Place then I obſerve, That an immortal Life in this World, is not the Original Right of earthly Creatures, but was wholly owing to the Grace and Favour of God. I call that an Original Right which is founded in the Nature of Things; for otherwiſe, properly ſpeaking, no Creatures have any Right, either to Being, or to Subſiſtence, which is a Continuance in Being: It is the Goodneſs and the Power of God, which both made the World, and upholds and ſuſtains all Things in Being. And therefore *Plato* confeſſes, That the inferior Gods, thoſe immortal Spirits, which he thought worthy of Divine Honours, were both made by the Supreme God, and did ſubſiſt by his Will: For he who made all Things, can annihilate them again when he pleaſes; and therefore their Subſiſtence is as much owing to the Divine Goodneſs, as their Creation. But yet there

is

is a great Difference between the natural Gift and Bounty of God, and what is supernatural, or above the Nature of Things: What God makes by Nature immortal, so that it has no Principles of Mortality in its Constitution, Immortality may be said to be its natural Right, because it is by Nature immortal, as Spirits and the Souls of Men are. And in this Case it would be thought very hard, that a whole Race of immortal Beings should be made mortal for the Sin of one; which would be to deprive them of their natural Right to Immortality, without their own Fault. But when any Creature is immortal, not by Nature, but by supernatural Grace, God may bestow this supernatural Immortality upon what Conditions he pleases, and take the Forfeiture of it when he sees fit. And this was the Case of Man in Innocence: His Body was not by Nature immortal; for a Body made of Dust, will naturally resolve into Dust again; and therefore without a supernatural Power, an earthly Body must die; for which Reason God provided a Remedy against Mortality, the Tree of Life, which he planted in Paradise, and without which Man could not be immortal: So that Mortality was a necessary Consequence of his losing Paradise; for when he was banished from the Tree of Life, he could have no Remedy nor Preservative against Death. Now I suppose, no Man will question, but God might very

justly

justly turn *Adam* out of Paradise for his Disobedience, and then he must die, and all his Posterity die in him: For he being by Nature mortal, must beget mortal Children; and having forfeited the Tree of Life, he and his Posterity, who are all shut out of Paradise with him, must necessarily die: Which takes nothing from them, to which any Man had a Right, (for no Man had a natural Right to Paradise, or the Tree of Life) but only leaves them to those Laws of Mortality, to which an earthly Creature is naturally subject. God had promised Paradise and the Tree of Life to no Man, but to *Adam* himself, whom he created and placed in Paradise; and therefore he took nothing away from any Man, but from *Adam*, when he thrust him out of Paradise. Children indeed must follow the Conditions of their Parents. Had *Adam* preserved his Right to the Tree of Life, we had enjoyed it too; but he forfeiting it, we lost it in him, and in him die: We lost, I say, not any thing that we had a Right to, but such a supernatural Privilege, as we might have had, had he preserved his Innocence: And this is a sufficient Vindication of the Justice of God in it. He has done us no Injury; we are by Nature mortal Creatures, and he leaves us in that mortal State: And to withdraw Favours upon a reasonable Provocation, is neither hard nor unjust.

II. For

II. For we must consider farther, when Sin was once entered into the World, an immortal Life here became impossible, without a constant Series of Miracles. *Adam* had sinned, and thereby corrupted his own Nature, and therefore must necessarily propagate a corrupt Nature to his Posterity: His earthly Passions were broke loose, he now knew Good and Evil: and therefore was in the Hands of his own Counsel, to refuse or chuse the Good or Evil, And when the animal Life was once awakened in him, there was no great Dispute which way his Affections would incline: To be sure it is evident enough in his Posterity, whose boisterous Passions act such Tragedies in the World. Now suppose in a State of Innocence, that the Tree of Life would have preserved Men immortal, when no Man would injure himself nor another; when there was no Danger from wild Beasts, or any intemperate Air, or poisonous Herbs; yet, I suppose, no Man will say, but that even in Paradise itself, (could we suppose any such Thing) *Adam* might have been devoured by a Beast, or killed with a Stab at the Heart; or had there been any Poison there, it would have killed him, had he eaten or drunk it, or else he had another Kind of Body in Paradise than we have now, for I am sure that these Things would kill us: Consider then how impossible it is, that in this fallen apostate State, God should

should preserve Man immortal, without working Miracles every Minute: Men's Passions are now very unruly, and they fall out with one another, and will kill one another if they can; of which the World had a very early Example in *Cain*, who slew his Brother *Abel*; and all those Murthers and bloody Wars since that Day put this Matter out of Doubt: Now this can never be prevented, unless God should make our Bodies invulnerable, which a Body of Flesh and Blood cannot be without a Miracle: Some die by their own Hands, others by wild Beasts, others by evil Accidents; and there are so many Ways of destroying these brittle Bodies, that it is the greatest Wonder that they last so long. And yet *Adam*'s Body in Paradise was as very Earth, and as brittle as our Bodies are; but all this had been prevented, had Men continued innocent; they would not then have quarrelled or fought; they would not have died by their own Hands, nor drank themselves into a Fever, nor overloaded Nature with riotous Excesses; there had been no wild Beasts to devour, no infectious Air, or poisonous Herbs, and then the Tree of Life would have repaired all the Decays of Nature, and preserved a perpetual Youth; but in this State we are now, the Tree of Life could not preserve us immortal if a Sword or Poison can kill; which shews us how impossible it was, but that Sin and Death must come into the World together:

Man.

Man might have been immortal, had he never sinned; but brutish and ungovern'd Passions will destroy us without a Miracle. And therefore we have no Reason now to quarrel at the Divine Providence, that we are mortal, for in the ordinary Course of Providence, it is impossible it should be otherwise.

III. Considering what the State of this World necessarily is, since the Fall of Man, an immortal Life here is not desirable: No State ought to be immortal, if it be designed as an Act of Favour and Kindness, but what is completely happy; but this World is far enough from being such a State. Some few Years give wise Men enough of it, tho' they are not oppressed with any great Calamities; and there are a great many Miseries, which nothing but Death can give Relief to: This puts an End to the Sorrows of the Poor, of the Oppressed, of the Persecuted; it is a Haven of Rest after all the Tempests of a troublesome World; it knocks off the Prisoner's Shackles, and sets him at Liberty; it dries up the Tears of the Widows and Fatherless; it eases the Complaints of a hungry Belly, and naked Back; it tames the proudest Tyrants, and restores Peace to the World; it puts an End to all our Labours, and supports Men under their present Adversities, especially when they have a Prospect of a better Life after this. The Labour and the Misery

So that considering the fallen State of Man, it was not fitting, it was not for the Good of Mankind, that they should be immortal here. Both the Wisdom, and Goodness, and Justice of God required that Man should die; which is an abundant Justification of this Divine Decree, That *it is appointed for Men once to die.*

V. As a farther Justification of the Divine Goodness in this, we may observe, that before God pronounced that Sentence on *Adam*, *Dust thou art, and to Dust thou shalt return;* he expressly promis'd, that the *seed of the woman shall bruise the serpent's head*, Gen. iii. 15. in his Curse upon the Serpent, who beguiled *Eve: I will put enmity between thee and the woman, and between thy seed and her seed; it shall bruise thy head, and thou shalt bruise his heel.* Which contains the Promise of sending Christ into the World, who *by death should destroy him who had the power of death, that is, the Devil; and deliver them, who through fear of death, were all their life-time subject to bondage;* Heb. ii. 14, 15. *i. e.* before he denounces the Sentence of Death against Man he promises a Saviour and Deliverer, who should triumph over Death, and raise our dead Bodies out of the Dust, immortal and glorious. Here is a most admirable Mixture of Mercy and Judgment! Man had forfeited an earthly Immortality, and must die;
but

but before God would denounce the Sentence of Death againſt him, he promiſes to raiſe up his dead Body again to a new and endleſs Life. And have we any Reaſon to complain then, that God has dealt hardly with us, in involving us in the ſad Conſquences of *Adam*'s Sin, and expoſing us to a temporal Death, when he has promiſed to raiſe us up from the Dead again, and to beſtow a more glorious Immortality on us, which we ſhall never loſe? When Man had ſinned, it was neceſſary that he ſhould die, becauſe he could never be completely and perfectly happy in this World, as you have already heard: And the only poſſible Way to make him happy, was to tranſlate him into another World, and to beſtow a better Immortality on him. This God has done, and that in a very ſtupendious Way, by giving his own Son to die for us; and now we have little Reaſon to complain, that we all die in *Adam*, ſince we are made alive in Chriſt. To have died in *Adam*, never to have lived more, had indeed been very ſevere upon Mankind; but when Death ſignifies only a Neceſſity of going out of theſe Bodies, and living without them for ſome Time, in order to re-aſſume them again immortal and glorious, we have no Reaſon to think this any great Hurt. Nay, indeed, if we conſider Things rightly, the Divine Goodneſs has improved the Fall of *Adam* to the raiſing of Mankind to a more happy and perfect State.

G 4 For

For though Paradife, where God placed *Adam* in Innocence, was a happier State of Life than this World, freed from all the Diforders of a mortal Body, and from all the neceffary Cares and Troubles of this Life, yet you'll all grant that Heaven is a happier Place than an earthly Paradife; and therefore it is more for our Happinefs to be tranflated from Earth to Heaven, than to have lived always in an earthly Paradife. You will all grant, that the State of good Men, when they go out of thefe Bodies before the Refurrection, is a happier Life than Paradife was; for it is to *be with Chrift*, as St *Paul* tells us, *which is far better*, Phil. i. 23. And when our Bodies rife again from the Dead, you will grant they will be more glorious Bodies than *Adam*'s was in Innocence: For *the firft man was of the earth earthy, but the fecond man is the Lord from heaven*, 1 Cor. xv. 47. *Adam* had an earthly mortal Body, though it fhould have been immortal by Grace; but at the Refurrection our Bodies fhall be fafhioned like unto Chrift's moft glorious Body. *The righteous fhall fhine forth like the Sun in the kingdom of their Father: That as we have borne the image of the earthly, we fhall alfo bear the image of the heavenly*, 1 Cor. xv. 49. So that our Redemption by Chrift has infinitely the Advantage of *Adam*'s Fall, and we have no reafon to complain, That *by man came death, fince by man alfo came the refurrection of the dead*. That
St

St *Paul* might well magnify the Grace of God in our Redemption by Chriſt, above his Juſtice and Severity in puniſhing *Adam*'s Sin with Death, *Rom.* v. 15, 16, 17. *But not as the offence, ſo alſo is the free gift: For if thro' the offence of one, many be dead; much more the grace of God, and the gift by grace, which is by one man, Jeſus Chriſt, hath abounded unto many. And not as it was by one that ſinned, ſo is the gift: for the judgment was by one to condemnation; but the free gift is of many offences unto juſtification. For if by one man's offence, death reigned by one; much more they which receive abundance of grace, and of the gift of righteouſneſs, ſhall reign in life by one, Jeſus Chriſt.* Where the Apoſtle magnifies the Grace of God upon a fourfold Account. 1. That Death was the juſt reward of Sin, it came by *the offence of one*, and was an Act of Juſtice in God: Whereas our Redemption by Chriſt is the Gift of Grace, the free Gift, which we had no juſt Claim to. 2. That by Chriſt we are not only deliver'd from the Effects of *Adam*'s Sin, but from the Guilt of our own: *For tho' the judgment was by one to condemnation; the free gift is of many offences unto juſtification.* 3. That though we die in *Adam*, we are not barely made alive again in Chriſt, but *ſhall reign in life by one, Jeſus Chriſt*; which is a much happier Life than what we loſt in *Adam*. 4. That as we die by one Man's Offence, ſo we live by one too; *By the righteouſ-*
neſs

— — — — — — — — — gift comes upon all men unto — — — — — —. We have no reason to complain, that the Sin of *Adam* is imputed to us in Death, if the Righteousness of Christ purchase for us eternal Life. The first was a necessary Consequence of *Adam*'s losing Paradise; the second is wholly owing to the Grace of God.

Thus we see what it is that makes us mortal: God did not make Death; he created us in a happy and immortal State; but *by man sin entred into the world, and death by sin.* Whatever Aversion then we have to Death, should beget in us a greater Horror of Sin, which did not only at first make us mortal, but is to this Day both the Cause of Death, and the Sting of it. No Degree indeed of Virtue now can preserve us from dying; but yet Virtue may prolong our Lives, and make them happy while Sin very often hastens us to the Grave, and cuts us off in the very midst of our Days. An intemperate and luftful Man destroys the most vigorous Constitution of Body, dies of a Fever, or Dropsy, or Rottenness and Consumptions; others fall a Sacrifice to private Revenge, or publick Justice, or a Divine Vengeance, *for the wicked shall not live out half their Days.* However, setting aside some little natural Aversions, which are more easily conquer'd, and Death were a very innocent, harmless, nay, desirable Thing, did not Sin give a Sting to it, and terrify us with the Thoughts of that Judgment which is to follow. Quarrel not then at the Divine Juſtice in appointing Death; God is very good, as well as juſt in it; but vent all your Indignation againſt Sin; pull out this Sting of Death, and then you will ſee nothing but Smiles and Charms in it; that it is nothing but putting off theſe mortal Bodies; to reaſſume them again with all the Advantage of an immortal Youth. It is certain indeed we muſt die, this is appointed for us; and the very Certainty of our Death will teach us that Wiſdom which may help us to regain a better Immortality than we have loſt.

SECT. II.

How to improve this Conſideration, That we muſt certainly die.

FOR, 1. If it be certain that we muſt die, this ſhould teach us frequently to think of Death, to keep it always in our Eye and View. For, why ſhould we caſt off the Thoughts of that which will certainly come, eſpecially when it was ſo neceſſary to the good Government of our Lives, to remember that we muſt die? If we muſt die, I think it concerns us to take care, that we may die happily, and that depends upon our living well; and nothing has ſuch a powerful Influence upon the good Government of our Lives, as

the

the thoughts of Death. I have already shewed you what Wisdom Death will teach us; but no Man will learn this, who does not consider what it is to die; and no Man will practise it, who does not often remember that he must die: But he that lives under a constant Sense of Death, has a perpetual Antidote against the Follies and Vanities of this World, and a perpetual Spur to Virtue.

When such a Man finds his Desires after this World enlarge beyond, not only the Wants, but the Conveniencies of Nature, Thou Fool, says he to himself, What is the Meaning of all this? What kindles this insatiable Thirst of Riches? Why must there be no end of adding House to House, and Field to Field? Is this World thy Home? Is this thy abiding City? Dost thou hope to take up an eternal Rest here? Vain Man! Thou must shortly remove thy Dwelling, and then whose shall all these Things be? Death will shortly close thy Eyes, and then thou shalt not so much as see the God thou worshippest; the Earth shall shortly cover thee, and then thou shalt have thy Mouth and Belly full of Clay and Dust. Such Thoughts as these will cool our Desires to this present World: will make us contented when we have enough, and very charitable and liberal of what we can spare: For what should we do with more in this World, than will carry us through it? What better and wiser Use can we make of such

Riches

Riches as we cannot carry with us into the other World, than to return them thither before-hand in Acts of Piety and Charity, that we may receive the Rewards and Recompence of them in a better Life? That we may *make to ourselves friends of the mammon of unrighteousness, that when we fail they may receive us into everlasting habitations.*

When he finds his Mind begin to swell, and to increase as his Fortune and Honours do; Lord, thinks he, what a Bubble is this! which every Breath of Air can blow away? How vain a Thing is Man in his greatest Glory, who appears gay and beautiful, like a Flower in the Spring, and is as soon cut down and withered! Though we should meet with no Change in our Fortune here, yet we shall suddenly be removed out of this World; the Scene of this Life will change, and there is an End of earthly Greatness. And what a contemptible Mind is that, which is swell'd with dying Honours, which look big indeed, as a Body does which is swell'd out of all Proportion with a Dropsy or Tympany; but that is its Disease, not a natural Beauty. What am I better than the poorest Man who begs an Alms, unless I be wiser and more virtuous than he? Can Lands and Houses, great Places and Titles; Things which are not ours, and which we cannot keep, make such a mighty Difference between one Man and another? Are these the Riches? Are these
the

the Beauties and Glories of a Spirit? Are we not all made of the same Mould? Is not God the Father of us all; Muſt we not all die alike and lie down in the Duſt together? And can the different Parts we act in this World, which are not so long as the Scene of a Play, compared to an eternal Duration, make such a vaſt Difference between Men? This will make Men humble and modeſt in the higheſt Fortune, as minding them, that when they are got to the Top-round of Honour, if they keep from falling, yet they muſt be carried down again, and laid as low as the Duſt.

Thus when he finds the Body growing upon the Mind, and intoxicating it with the Love of senſual Pleaſures, he remembers that his Body muſt die, and all theſe Pleaſures muſt die with it; that they are indeed killing Pleaſures, which kill a mortal Body before its Time; that it does not become a Man who is but a Traveller in this World, but a Pilgrim and Stranger here, to ſtudy Eaſe, and Softneſs and Luxury; that a Soul which muſt live for ever, ſhould ſeek after more laſting Pleaſures, which may survive the Funeral of the Body, and be a Spring of raviſhing Joys when he is ſtripp'd of Fleſh and Blood. Theſe are the Thoughts which the Conſideration of Death will ſuggeſt to us, as I have already ſhew'd you. And it is impoſſible for a Man, who has always theſe Thoughts at hand, to be much impoſed on by the Pageantry

antry of this World, by the transient Honours and Pleasures of it.

It is indeed, I think, a very impracticable Rule, which some Men give, To live always as if we were to die the next Moment. Our Lives should always be as innocent, as if we were immediately to give up our Accounts to God; but it is impossible to have always those sensible Apprehensions of Death about us, which we have when we see it approaching. But though we cannot live as if we were immediately to die, (which would put an end not only to all innocent Mirth, but to all the necessary Business of the World, which I believe no dying Man will concern himself for) yet we may, and we ought to live as those who must certainly die, and ought to have these Thoughts continually about us, as a Guard upon our Actions. For whatever is of such mighty Consequence to us, as Death is, if it be certain, ought always to give Laws to our Behaviour and Conversation.

2*dly*, If it be certain we must die, the very first Thing we ought to do in this World, after we come to Years of Understanding, should be to prepare for Death, that whenever Death comes, we may be ready for it.

This, I confess, is not according to the Way of this World; for dying is usually the last thing they take care of. This is thought a little unreasonble, while Men are young and healthful,

healthful, and vigorous. But befides the Uncertainty of our Lives, and that it is poffible while we delay, Death may feize on us before we are provided for it; and then we muft be miferable for ever; [which I fhall fpeak to under the next Head] I doubt not but to convince every confidering Man, that an early Preparation for Death, is the very beft Means to make our Lives happy in this World, while we do continue here. Nor fhall I urge here, how a Life of Holinefs and Virtue, which is the beft and only Preparation for Death, tends to make us happy in this World, delivers us from all thofe Mifchiefs which the Wildnefs and Giddinefs of Youth, and the more confirmed Debaucheries of riper Years, expofe Men to: For this is properly the Commendation of Virtue, not of an early Preparation for Death. And yet this is really a great Engagement and Motive to prepare betimes for Death, fince fuch a Preparation for Death will put us to no greater Hardfhips and Inconveniencies, than the Practice of fuch Virtues as will prolong our Lives, preferve or increafe our Fortunes, give us Honour and Reputation in the World, and make us beloved both by God and Men. But fetting afide thefe Things, there are two Advantages of an early Preparation for Death, which contribute more to our Happinefs than all the World befides. 1. That it betimes delivers us from the Fears of Death, and confequently

from

from most other Fears. 2. That it supports us under all the Troubles and Calamities of this Life.

1. It betimes delivers us from the Fears of Death: And indeed it is then only a Man begins to live, when he is got above the Fears of Death. Were Men thoughtful and considerate, Death would hang over them in all their Mirth and Jollity, like a fatal Sword by a single Hair; it would sowre all their Enjoyments, and strike Terror into their Hearts and Looks. But the Security of most Men is, that they put off the Thoughts of Death, as they do their Preparation for it: They live secure and free from Danger, only because they will not open their Eyes to see it. But these are such Examples as no wise Man will propose to himself, because they are not safe. And there are so many Occasions to put these Men in mind of Death, that it is a very hard thing not to think of it; and whenever they do, it chills their Blood and Spirits, and draws a black melancholy Veil over all the Glories in the World. How are such Men surprized when any Danger approaches? When Death comes within View, and shews his Scythe, and only some few Sands at the bottom of the Glass? This is a very frightful Sight to Men who are not prepared to die: And yet should they give themselves Liberty to think in what Danger they live every Minute, how many thousand Accidents may cut them

them off, which they can neither foresee nor prevent; Fear, and Horror, and Consternation, would be their constant Entertainment, 'till they could think of Death without Fear; 'till they were reconciled to the Thoughts of dying, by great and certain Hopes of a better Life after Death.

So that no Man can live happily, if he lives like a Man with his Thoughts and Reason and Consideration about him, but he who takes care betimes to prepare for Death and another World. 'Till this be done, a wise Man will see himself always in Danger, and then he must always fear. But he is a happy Man, who knows and considers himself to be mortal, and is not afraid to die. His Pleasures and Enjoyments are sincere and unmix'd, never disturb'd with a Hand-writing upon the Wall, nor with some secret Qualms and Misgivings of Mind, he is not terrified with present Dangers, at least not amazed and distracted with them. A Man who is deliver'd from the Fears of Death, fears nothing else in Excess but God. And Fear is so troublesome a Passion, that nothing is more for the Happiness of our Lives, than to be deliver'd from it.

2. As a Consequence of this, an early Preparation for Death will support Men under all the Troubles and Calamities of this Life. There are so many Troubles which Mankind are expos'd to in this World, that no Man must

muſt expect to eſcape them all; nay, there are a great many Troubles which are unſupportable to human Nature, which there can be no Relief for in this World. The Hopes and Expectations of a better Life are, in moſt Caſes, the ſafeſt Retreat. A Man may bear his preſent Sufferings with ſome Courage, when he knows that he ſhall quickly ſee an End of them, that Death will put an End to them, and place him out of their Reach. For *there the wicked ceaſe from troubling, and there the weary be at reſt; there the priſoners reſt together, they hear not the voice of the oppreſſor; the ſmall and great are there, and the ſervant is free from his maſter.* Job iii. 17, 18, 19.

So that in many Caſes the Thoughts and Expectations of Death is the only Thing that can ſupport us under preſent Sufferings; but while the Thoughts of Death itſelf are terrible to us, this will be a poor Comfort. Men who are under the Senſe of Guilt, are more afraid of Death than they are of all the Evils of this World. Whatever their preſent Sufferings are, they are not ſo terrible *as lakes of fire and brimſtone, the worm that never dieth, and the fire that never goeth out.* So that ſuch Men, while they are under the Fears and Terrors of Death, have nothing to ſupport them under preſent Miſeries. The next World, which Death puts us into the Poſſeſſion of, is a very delightful Proſpect to good Men;

Men; there they see the Rewards of their Labour and Sufferings, of their Faith and Patience. They can suffer Shame and Reproach, and *take joyfully the spoiling of their goods; since these light afflictions, which are but for a season, will work for them a far more exceeding and eternal weight of glory.* But Men who are not prepared to die, while they are afraid of Death, can find no Relief in the Thoughts of it, and therefore want the greatest Support that we can have in this Life against the Sufferings of it. The sooner we prepare to die, the sooner we are deliver'd from the Fears of Death; and then the Hope of a better Life will carry us chearfully thro' this World, whatever Storms we meet with.

3*dly*, Since we must certainly die, it makes it extremely reasonable to sacrifice our Lives to God, whenever he calls for them; that is, rather to chuse to die a little before our Time, than to renounce God, or to give his Worship to Idols, or any created Beings, or to corrupt the Faith and Religion of Christ. There are Arguments indeed enough to encourage Christians to Martyrdom, when God calls them to suffer for his sake: The Love of Christ in dying for us, is a sufficient Reason why we should chearfully die for him; and the great Rewards of Martyrdom, that glorious Crown which is reserved for such Conquerors, made the primitive Christians

ambitious

ambitious of it. It is certain there is no hurt in it: Nay, that it is a peculiar Favour to die for Christ; because those Persons who are most dear to him, were crowned with Martyrdom. But our present Argument shews us, at what an easy Rate we may purchase so glorious a Crown; for we part with nothing for it: We die for God, and we must die whether we die Martyrs or not. And what Man then, who knows he must die, and believes the Rewards of Martyrdom, can think it so terrible to die a Martyr? No good Christian can think that he loses any thing by the Bargain, to exchange this Life for a better; for as many Years as he goes sooner out of this World, than he should have done by the Course of Nature, so many Years he gets sooner to Heaven; and I suppose, that is no great Loss. It is indeed a noble Expression of our Love to God, and our entire Obedience and Subjection to him, and of a perfect Trust in him, to part with our Lives for his Sake? But what can a Man, who knows he must die, do less for God than this; to part with a Life which he cannot keep, willingly to lay down a Life for God, which would shortly be taken from him whether he will or not?

4*thly*, This shews us also, what little Reason we have to be afraid of the Power of Men. The utmost they can do, is to kill the Body;

a mortal

a mortal Body, which will die whether they kill it or not: Which is no mighty Argument of Power, no more than it is to break a brittle Glass; nor any great Hurt to us, no more than it is to die, which we are all born to, and which is no Injury to a good Man. And therefore our Saviour's Counsel is very reasonable, *Luke* xii. 4, 5. *Be not afraid of them who kill the Body, and after that have no more that they can do; but I forewarn you whom you shall fear: Fear him, which after he hath killed, hath power to cast into hell; yea, I say unto you, fear him.*

This is very reasonable, when the Fear of God and Men is opposed to each other, which is the only Case our Saviour supposes. No Man ought foolishly to fling away his Life, nor to provoke and affront Princes, who have the Power of Life and Death: This is not to die like a Martyr, but like a Fool, or a Rebel. But when a Prince threatens Death, and God threatens Damnation, then our Saviour's Counsel takes place, not to fear Men, but God. For indeed God's Power in this is equal to Men's at least. Men can kill, for Men are mortal, and may be killed; and this is only for a mortal Creature to die a little out of Order: But God can kill too; and thus far the Case is the same. It is true, most Men are of the mind, in such a Case, rather to trust God than Men; because he does not always punish in this World,

nor

nor execute a speedy Vengeance. And yet when our Saviour takes notice, That God kills as well as Men, it seems to intimate to us, that such Apostates, who rather chuse to provoke God than Men, may meet with their Deserts in this World: For no Man is secure that God will not punish him in this World; and Apostates of all others have least Reason to expect it. Those who renounce God for fear of Men, are the fittest Persons to be made Examples of a sudden Vengeance. But then when Men have killed, they can do no more; they cannot kill the Soul. And here the Power of God and Men is very unequal; for when he has killed, he can cast both Body and Soul into Hell-fire. This is a very formidable Power indeed; and we have Reason to fear him: But the Power of Men, who can only kill a mortal Body, is not very terrible; it ought not to fright us into any Sin, which will make us obnoxious to that more terrible Power which can destroy the Soul.

CHAP. III.

Concerning the Time of our Death, and the proper Improvement of it.

LET us now confider the Time of our Death, which is once, but when uncertain.

Now when I fay the Time of our Death is uncertain, I need not tell you, That I mean only it is uncertain to us; that is, That no Man knows when he fhall die, for God certainly knows when we fhall die, becaufe he knows all things; and therefore with refpect to the Fore-knowledge of God, the Time of our Death is certain:

Thus much is certain as to Death, That we muft all die; and it is certain alfo that Death is not far off, becaufe we know our Lives are very fhort. Before the Flood Men lived many hundred Years: But it is a great while now fince the *Pfalmift* obferved, that the ordinary Term of human Life had very narrow Bounds fet to it; *The days of our years are threefcore years and ten; and if by reafon of ftrength, they be fourfcore years, yet is their ftrength labour and forrow: for it is foon cut off, and we fly away.* Pfalm xc. 10. There are fome Exceptions from this general Rule, but this

this is the ordinary Period of human Life, when it is spun out to the greatest Length; and therefore within this Term we may reasonably expect it; for in the ordinary Course of Nature, our Bodies are not made to last much longer.

Thus far we are certain: But then, how much of this Time we shall run out, how soon, or how late we shall die, we know not; for we see no Age exempted from Death: Some expire in the Cradle, and at their Mothers Breasts; others in the Heat and Vigour of Youth; others survive to a decrepit Age, and, it may be, follow their whole Family to their Graves. Death very often surprizeth us, when we least think of it, without giving us any Warning of it's Approach; and that is Proof enough, that the Time of our Death is unknown and uncertain to us.

But these Things deserve to be particularly discoursed; and therefore with reference to the Time of our Death, I shall observe these four Things; not so much to explain them, for most of them are plain enough of themselves, as to improve them for the Government of our Lives.

 I. That the general Period of human Life, which is the same Thing with the Time of our Death, is fix'd and determined by God.

II. That

II. That the particular Time of every Man's Death, though it be foreknown by God, who foreknows all Things; yet it does not appear, that it is peremptorily decreed and determined by God.

III. That the particular Time when any of us shall die, is unknown and uncertain to us.

IV. That we must die but once: *It is appointed for all men once to die.*

SECT. I.

That the general Period of human Life is fix'd and determined by GOD, and that is but very short.

I. THAT the general Period of human Life, which is the same Thing with the Time of our Death, is fix'd and determin'd by God; that is, there is a Time set to human Life, beyond which no Man shall live, as *Job* speaks, *Job* xiv. 5. *His days are determined, the number of his months are with thee; thou hast appointed his bounds that he cannot pass.* Which does not refer to the Period of every particular Man's Life, but is spoken of Men in general, that there are fix'd Bounds set to human Life, which no Man can exceed.

What these Bounds are, God has not expressly declar'd, but that must be learn'd from Observation.

Observation. Such a Time as most commonly puts a Period to Men's Lives who live longest, may generally pass for the common Measure of human Life, though there may be some few Exceptions.

Before the Flood no Man lived a thousand Years; and therefore we may conclude, That the longest Term of human Life, after the Sentence of Death was passed on Man, was confined within a thousand Years. *Methuselah*, who was the longest Liver, lived but nine hundred sixty-nine Years, and he died; so that no Man ever lived a thousand Years: And comparing this Observation with that Promise of a thousand Years Reign with Christ, which is called the first Resurrection, and is the Portion only of Martyrs and Confessors, and pure and sincere Christians, *Rev.* xx. I have been apt to conclude, That to live a thousand Years, is the Privilege only of immortal Creatures; that if *Adam* had continued innocent, he should have lived no longer on Earth, but have been translated to Heaven without dying; for this thousand Years Reign of the Saints with Christ, whatever that signifies, seems to be intended as a Reparation of that Death which they fell under by *Adam's* Sin: But then these thousand Years do not put an End to the Happiness of these glorious Saints, but they are immortal Creatures; and though this Reign with Christ continues but a thousand Years, their Happiness

Happiness shall have no End, tho' the Scene may change and vary: *For over such men the second death hath no power.* Or else this thousand Years Reign with Christ must signify an eternal and unchangeable Kingdom, a thousand Years being a certain Earnest of Immortality; but there is an unanswerable Objection against that, because we read of the expiring of these thousand Years, and what shall come after them, even the final Judgment of all the World. But this is a great Mystery, which we must not hope perfectly to understand, 'till we see the blessed Accomplishment of it.

But though before the Flood some Persons lived very near the thousand Years, yet after the Flood the Term of Life was much shorten'd: Some think this was done by God, when he pronounced that Sentence, *Gen.* vi. 3. *And the Lord said, My Spirit shall not always strive with man, for that he also is flesh, yet his days shall be an hundred and twenty years.* As if God had then decreed, that the Life of Man should not exceed an hundred and twenty Years. But this does not agree with that Account we have of Mens Lives after the Flood; for not only *Noah* and his Sons, who were with him in the Ark, lived much longer than this after the Flood; *Arphaxad* lived five hundred and thirty Years, *Salah* four hundred and three Years, *Eber* four hundred and thirty Years, and *Abraham* himself
a hundred

a hundred seventy-five Years; and therefore this hundred and twenty Years cannot refer to the ordinary Term of Man's Life, but to the Continuance of God's Patience with that wicked World, before he would bring the Flood upon them to destroy that corrupt Generation of Men; that is, That he would bear with them a hundred and twenty Years before he would send the Flood to destroy them. But afterwards by degrees Life was shorten'd, insomuch, that though *Moses* himself lived a great deal longer, yet if the xcth *Psalm* was composed by him, as the Title tells us it was, the ordinary Term of Life in his Days was but threescore and ten, or fourscore Years, *ver.* 10. *The days of our years are threescore years and ten; and if by reason of strength they be fourscore years, yet is their strength labour and sorrow; so soon passeth it away, and it is gone.* And this has continued the ordinary Measure of Life ever since; which is so very short, that *David* might well say, *Behold thou hast made my days as a handbreadth, and mine age is as nothing before thee: verily every man at his best estate is altogether vanity.* Psal. xxxix. 5.

I shall not scrupulously enquire into the Reason of this great Change, why our Lives are reduced into so narrow a Compass: Some will not believe that it was so, but think that there is a Mistake in the Manner of the Account; that when they are said to live eight

or

or nine hundred Years, they computed their Years by the Moon, not by the Sun; that is, their Years were Months, twelve of which make but one of our Years; and then indeed the longest Livers of them did not live so long as many Men do at this Day; for *Methuselah* himself, who lived nine hundred sixty-nine Years, according to this Computation of Months for Years, lived but fourscore Years and five Months. But it is very absurd to imagine, that *Moses* should use two such different Accounts of Time, that sometimes by a Year he should mean no more than a Month, and sometimes twelve Months, without giving the least Notice of it, which is unpardonable in any Historian: And therefore others complain much that they were not born in those Days, when the Life of Man was prolonged for so many hundred Years: There had been some Comfort in living then, when they enjoyed all the Vigour and Gaiety of Youth, and could relish the Pleasures of Life for seven, eight, or nine hundred Years. A Blessing which Men would purchase at any rate in our Days: But now we can scarce turn ourselves about in the World, but we are admonished by grey Hairs, or the sensible Decays of Nature, to prepare for our Winding-Sheet. And therefore, for the farther Improvement of this Argument, I shall, 1. shew you, What little Reason we have to complain of the Shortness of Life. 2. What what wise Use we are to make of it.

SECT. II.

What little Reason we have to complain of the Shortness of human Life.

WHAT little Reason we have to complain of the Shortness of Life, and the too hasty Approaches of Death to us; for, 1. Such a long Life is not reconcileable with the present State of the World. And, 2dly, Our Lives are long enough for all the wise Purposes of Living.

1. Such a long Life is not reconcileable with the present State of the World. What the State of the World was before the Flood, in what Manner they lived, and how they employed their Time, we cannot tell, for *Moses* has given no Account of it; but taking the World as it is, and as we find it, I dare undertake to convince those Men who are most apt to complain of the Shortness of Life, that it would not be for the general Happiness of Mankind to have it much longer: For, 1. The World is at present very unequally divided; some have a large Share and Portion of it, others have nothing, but what they earn by very hard Labour, or extort from other Men's Charity by their restless Importunities, or gain by more ungodly Arts: Now, though the Rich and Prosperous, who have the World at Command, and live in
Ease

Ease and Pleasure, would be very well contented to spend some hundred Years in this World; yet I should think fifty or threescore Years abundantly enough for Slaves and Beggars, enough to spend in Hunger and Want, in a Goal and a Prison. And those who are so touchy as not to think this enough, owe a great deal to the Wisdom and Goodness of God, that he dies: So that the greatest Part of Mankind have great Reason to be contented with the Shortness of Life, because they have no Temptation to wish it longer.

2ly. The present State of this World requires a more quick Succession: The World is pretty well peopled, and is divided among its present Inhabitants: and but very few, in comparison, as I observed before, have any considerable Share in the Division: Now let us but suppose that all our Ancestors, who lived an hundred, or two hundred Years ago, were alive still, and possessed their old Estates and Honours, what had become of this present Generation of Men, who have now taken their Places, and make as great a Show and Bustle in the World as they did? And if you look back three, or four, or five hundred Years, the Case is still so much the worse; the World would be over-peopled, and where there is one poor miserable Man now, there must have been five hundred, or the World must have been common, and all Men reduced to the same Level; which I believe the rich and happy People, who are so fond of long Life, would not like very well. This would utterly undo our young prodigal Heirs, were their Hopes of Succession three or four hundred Years off, who, as short as Life is now, think their Fathers make very little Haste to their Graves: This would spoil their Trade of spending their Estates before they have them, and make them live a dull sober Life whether they would or no; and such a Life, I know, they don't think worth having: And therefore, I hope, at least, they will not make the Shortness of their Fathers Lives an Argument against Providence. And yet such Kind of Sparks as these, are commonly the Wits that set up for Atheism, and, when it is put into their Heads, quarrel with every Thing, which they fondly conceive will weaken the Belief of a God, and a Providence, and among other Things, with the Shortness of Life; which they have little Reason to do, when they so often out-live their Estates.

3*dly*, The World is very bad as it is, so bad, that good Men scarce know how to spend fifty or threescore Years in it; but consider how bad it would probably be, were the Life of Man extended to six, seven, or eight hundred Years. If so near a Prospect of the other World, as forty or fifty Years, cannot restrain Men from the greatest Villanies, what would they do, if they could as reasonably suppose

Death to be three or four hundred Years off? If Men make such Improvements in Wickedness in twenty or thirty Years, What would they in hundreds? And what a blessed Place then would this World be to live in? We see in the old World, when the Life of Man was drawn out to so great a Length, the Wickedness of Mankind grew so insufferable, that it repented God he had made Man; and he resolved to destroy that whole Generation, excepting *Noah* and his Family. And the most probable Account that can be given, how they came to grow so universally wicked, is the long and prosperous Lives of such wicked Men, who by degrees corrupted others, and they others, 'till there was but one righteous Family left, and no other Remedy left, but to destroy them all; leaving only that righteous Family as the Seed and future Hopes of the new World.

And when God had determined in Himself and promised to *Noah*, never to destroy the World again by such an universal Destruction, 'till the last and final Judgment, it was necessary, by degrees, to shorten the Lives of Men, which was the most effectual Means to make them more governable, and to remove bad Examples out of the World; which would hinder the spreading of the Infection, and people and reform the World again by new Examples of Piety and Virtue. For when there are such quick Successions of Men, there are

few

few Ages but have some great and brave Examples, which give a new and better Spirit to the World.

Many other Things might be added, to convince those who complain of the Shortness of human Life, that it would be no desirable Thing, as the State of the World now is, to live seven or eight hundred Years in it: But this, I suppose, is enough, If I can make good the second Thing I propos'd, That our Lives are long enough for all the wise Purposes of living.

Now I will not promise myself to satisfy all Men in this Matter; for those who think it the only End of living, to eat and drink, and enjoy the more impure Delights of Flesh and Sense, will never be satisfy'd, that threescore and ten Years are as good as eight or nine hundred for this Purpose; for the longer they enjoy these Pleasures, and the oftener they repeat them, the better it is. But these Men ought to be convinced that this is not the true End of Living; that these are only Means to preserve Life, which God has sweetened with such proper Satisfactions, or made the Neglect of them so uneasy and painful, that no Man might forget to take care to preserve himself. But Man was made at first for higher and nobler Ends; and since by the Sin of *Adam* we are all become mortal, this Life is not for itself, but in order to a better Life.

We come into this World, not to stay here, or to take up our Abode and Rest; for then indeed the longer we lived the better. But this World is only a State of Trial and Discipline, to exercise our Virtues, to perfect our Minds, to prepare and qualify ourselves for the more pure, and refin'd, and spiritual Enjoyments of the other World. We come into this World, not so much to enjoy, as to conquer it, and to triumph over it, to baffle its Temptations, to despise its Flatteries, and to endure its Terrors: And if we live long enough to do this, we live long enough; and ought to thank God, that our Work, and Labour, and Temptations, are at an End. For what labouring Man is not glad that his Work is over, and he may go to Rest? What Mariner is not glad that he has weathered all Storms, and steered a safe Course to his desired Haven?

There are two Things necessary to the Improvement of our Minds, Knowledge and Virtue: And as God has shorten'd our Lives, so he has shorten'd our Work too, and given us a more easy and compendious Way to both.

Knowledge indeed is an infinite and endless Thing; and it is impossible throroughly to satisfy that Appetite in great and generous Minds, in this blind and obscure State of Life: But the Comfort is, all the Knowledge that is necessary to carry us to Heaven, is now plain and easy, and will not take up many

ny Years to learn it; for, *This is life eternal, to know God, and Jesus Christ whom he hath sent*; which is plainly revealed to us in the Gospel. And when we get to Heaven, we shall quickly understand all the Difficulties of Nature and Providence, in another manner than the greatest Philosophers do now, or can do, though they should live many hundred Years.

And as for Virtue, we have as short and easy a Way to it. The plainest and most perfect Precepts, the most admirable Examples, the most encouraging and inviting Promises; and, which is more than all, the most powerful Assistances of the Divine Spirit to renew and sanctify us: And he who is not reformed by these divine and supernatural Methods of Grace, in forty or fifty Years, is not likely to be the better for them, though he should live to *Methuselah*'s Age.

As for doing Good, I confess, the longer a good Man lives, the more Good he will do, and make himself the more useful to the World. But this is God's Care; and whenever he calls him out of the World, he excuses him from doing any more Good in it.

The Truth is, nothing could be more improper under the State of the Gospel, than such a long Life as worldly Men are very fond of. For our Saviour has taught us, to expect Persecutions and Sufferings for his Name; and this is very often the Portion of true and sincere Christians; that St *Paul* could say, *If in this Life only we had hope, we were of all men the most miserable.* Thanks be to God it is not always so; but when it is, it would be too great a Temptation for human Nature, to live some hundred Years in a State of Persecution; as they might, if they and the persecuting Prince should live so long.

Nay, such a long Life as these Men talk of, would greatly weaken the Promises and Threatenings of the Gospel; which are all absent and unseen Things, to be expected in the other World. But if the next World were so many hundred Years off, both the Promises and Threatenings of it would lose their Effect upon the Generality of Mankind.

Nay, it might be thought very hard upon good Men, who are taught by the Gospel of Christ to live above this World, and to have a very mean Opinion of, and a great Indifferency to, all the Delights of it, to live so many hundred Years in it; not so much to enjoy it, as to despise it, and to contend with it. And it is no less hard for Men, who are transported with the ravishing Hopes and Expectations of a better Life, whose Hearts and Conversations are already in Heaven, to be kept so long out of it. This is a severe Trial of their Patience: For Hope, when it is so long delayed, is a very troublesome and uneasy Passion; and though few Men long to die, yet a great many good Men do very impatiently

patiently long to be in Heaven, and can be contented, whenever God pleaſes, to ſubmit to dying, though with ſome natural Reluctancy, that they may get to Heaven. In ſhort, this Life is long enough for a Race, for a Warfare, for a Pilgrimage: It is long enough to fight and contend with this World, and all the Temptations of it: It is long enough to know this World, to diſcover the Vanity of it, and to live above it. It is long enough, by the Grace of God, to purge and refine our Minds, and to prepare ourſelves to live for ever in God's Preſence. And when we are in any meaſure prepared for Heaven, and poſſeſſed with great and paſſionate Deſires of it, we ſhall think it a great deal too long to be kept out of it.

SECT. III.

What Uſe to make of the fix'd Term of human Life.

II. LET us conſider what wiſe Uſe is to be made of this. And here are two Things diſtinctly to be conſider'd. 1. That the general Term of human Life is fix'd and determin'd by God. 2. That this common Term and Period of Life, at the utmoſt Extent of it, is but very ſhort.

1. That the general Term of human Life is fixed and determined by God. And this is capable of very wiſe Improvements. For,

1. When

1. When we know that we cannot live above threescore or fourscore Years, or some few Years over or under, we should not extend our Hopes, and Expectations, and Designs beyond this Term. 2. We should frequently count our Days, and observe how our Lives waste, and draw near to Eternity. 3. When this Period draws nigh, and Death comes within View, it more especially concerns us to apply ourselves to a more serious and solemn Preparation for Death.

1. We should not extend our Hopes, and Expectations, and Designs beyond this Term, which God has fix'd for the Conclusion of our Lives: We should not live as if we were immortal Creatures, who are never to die; for if God hath set Bounds to our Lives, it is absurd for us to expect to live any longer, unless we hope to alter the Decrees of Heaven.

And yet it is more absurd, if it be possible, to extend our Hopes and Desires, our Projects and Designs for this World, beyond the Term of our living here; for how unreasonable is it for us to trouble ourselves about this World longer than we are like to continue in it? And yet if this were observed, it would ease us of a great deal of Labour and Care, and deliver the World from those great Troubles and Disorders, which the Designs and Projects for future Ages create.

Men might see some End of their Labours, and of their Cares, of increasing Riches, and

adding

adding House to House, and Field to Field, did they stint their Desires with their Lives, did they consider how long they were to live, and what is a sufficient and necessary Provision for their Continuance here: Whereas now the Generality of Mankind drudge on to the last Moment they have to live, and still heap up Riches till they know no End of them, as if their Lives and their Enjoyments of them were to have no End neither.

The only tolerable Excuse that can be made for this, is the Care of Posterity, to leave a liberal Provision for Children, that they may live happily after us: But this indeed is rather an Excuse than a Reason; for thus we see it is, when there is no such Reason for it; when Men have no Children to provide for, nor it may be any Relations, for whom they are much concern'd; or when they have a sufficient Provision for all their Children, to encourage their Industry and Virtue, though not to maintain them in Idleness and Vice, which no wise and good Father would desire. Nay, it may be, when they have no other Heir to an overgrown Estate, but either a Daughter, whose Fortune may make her a rich Prey, as is too often seen; or a prodigal Son, who is ruined already by the Expectation of so great a Fortune; and will quickly be even with his Fortune, and ruin that when he has it.

A competent Provision for Children is a just Reason to continue our Industry, though
we

we have enough for ourselves, as long as we live; but to make them rich and great, is not. The Piety and Charity of Parents, which entails a Blessing upon their Posterity, and an industrious and virtuous Education of Children, is a better Inheritance for them than a great Estate: But Men, who are so intent to the very last upon increasing their Estates, seldom do it for any other Reason, but to satisfy their own insatiable Thirst, which is to hoard up Riches for a Time when they can't enjoy them, to provide for their living in this World a much longer Time than they know they can possibly live in it. This is much greater Folly than the Man in the Parable was guilty of, whose Ground brought forth plentifully, and he pulled down his Barns, and built greater, and *said to his soul, Soul, thou hast much goods laid up for many years, take thine ease, eat, drink, and be merry.* He was so wise as to know when he had enough, and when it was fit to retire and take his Ease: Yet God said unto him, *Thou fool, this night shall thy soul be required of thee; and then whose shall all these things be, which thou hast provided?* Luke xii. 16, &c.

Thus, how big are most Men with Projects and Designs, which there is little Hope should ever take effect while they live? Especially aspiring Monarchs, and busy Politicians, who draw the Scheme, and frame their Design of an universal Empire, thro' a long Series of Events;

Events; or meditate Changes and Alterations of Government, of the Laws and Religion of a Nation, by infenfible Steps and Methods; which, though it were never fo hopeful a Project, they can't hope to live to fee effected; and therefore exceed their own Bounds, and trouble the World at prefent, with what no Body now living may ever be concerned in: They undertake to govern the World when they are dead and gone; whereas every Age brings forth new Projects and Counfels, as it does a new Generation of Men; and new Scenes of Affairs, and a new Set of Politicians: Would but Men confine their Cares and Projects within the Bounds of their own Lives, and mind only what concerns themfelves, and their own Times, they would live more at Eafe, and the World enjoy more Peace and Quiet than now it is ever likely to do. And yet one would think this very reafonable, not to concern ourfelves about the World any longer than we are likely to live in it; to do no Injury to Pofterity as near as we can, and to do what Good we can for them, without difturbing the prefent Peace and good Government of the World; but to leave the Care of the next Age to thofe who fhall fucceed, and to that good Providence which governs and takes care of all Ages and Generations of Men.

2. Since we know the common Period of human Life, we fhould frequently count our
Days,

Days, and observe how our Lives waste, and draw near to Eternity. Our Time slides away insensibly, and few Men take notice how it goes; they find their Strength and Vigour continue without any Decay, and they reckon upon living threescore and ten, or fourscore Years; but seldom consider that it may be thirty or forty years are already gone; that is, the best half of their Lives. They put a Cheat upon themselves by computing the whole Duration of their Lives, without considering how much of this is already past, and how little of it is to come; which if Men should seriously think of, they would not be so apt to flatter themselves with a long Life; for no Man accounts twenty or thirty Years a long Life, and that is the most they have to live now, tho' they should attain to the longest Period of human Life; much less could they flatter themselves with a long Life, when they could not probably reckon above fifteen or ten Years to come. And would Men observe how their Lives shorten every Day, this, if any thing, would make them grow chary of their Time, and begin to think of living; that is, of minding the true Ends and Purposes of Life; of doing the Work for which they came into the World, and which they must do before they die, or they are miserable for ever.

3. When Men draw near the End of their Reckoning, nay, it may be are past the common

mon Reckoning of Mankind, it more especially concerns them to apply themselves to a more serious and solemn Preparation for Death: For how vigorous soever their Age is, Death cannot be far off; it would be unpardonable in them to be deceived with the Hopes of living much longer, who have already attained to the common Period of human Life, and are in the Borders and Confines, nay, in the very Quarters of Death, and have already, if I may so speak, borrowed some Years from the other World.

Now when I speak of such Mens preparing for Death, I do not mean, that they should then begin to think of dying; that is a great deal of the latest to begin such a Work; tho' if they have not done it before, it is without Doubt high Time to begin it then, in the last Minute of their Lives, and to do what they can in that little Time that remains, to obtain their Pardon of God for spending a long Life in Sin and Vanity, and in a Forgetfulness of their Maker and Redeemer.

But that which I now intend, concerns those who have thought of dying long before, and governed their Lives under the Conduct and Influence of such Thoughts; and therefore are not wholly unprepared for Death, but are ready to welcome it whenever it comes: But there is a decent Way of meeting Death which becomes such Men, which I call a more solemn Preparation for it; that is, when

when their Condition and Circumstances of Life will permit, to take a timely Leave of the World, and to withdraw from the Noise and Business of it; when they are placed just in the Confines of both Worlds, to direct their Faces wholly to that World whither they are going, to spend the little Remains of their Lives in conversing with themselves, with God, and with the other World.

1. In conversing with themselves; which, God knows, very few Men do, while they are engaged in the Business of this World; the Cares of Life, or the Pleasures of it, our Families, or our Friends, or Strangers themselves, take us from ourselves. And therefore it is fit before Men go out of this World, that they should recover the Possession of themselves, and grow a little more acquainted and intimate with themselves; that they should retire from the World to take a more thorough Review of their Lives and Actions, what they have still to do to make their Peace with God, and their own Consciences: Whether there be any Sin which they have not thoroughly repented of, and heartily begged God's Pardon for; any Injury they have done their Neighbour, for which they have not made sufficient Restitution and Reparation: Whether they have any Quarrel with any Man, which is not composed and reconciled: Whether there is any Part of their Duty, which they have formerly too much neglected;

lected; as Charity to the Poor; the wise Education and Instruction of their Children and Families; and to apply themselves to a more diligent Discharge of it: What Distempers there are in their Minds, which still need to be rectified: What Graces are weakest; what Passions are most disorderly and unmortified; and to apply proper Remedies to them.

This is an excellent Preparation for Death, because it will give us great Hope and Assurance in dying. It gives us Peace and Satisfaction in our own Minds, by a thorough Knowledge of our own State, and by rectifying whatever was amiss: It delivers our Conscience from guilty Fears, and disarms Death of its Sting and Terrors: For the Sting of Death is Sin; and when this Sting is pulled out, we have nothing else to contend with, but some little natural Aversions to dying, which are more easily conquered.

2. Thus in this preparatory Retirement from the World, we should spend great Portions of our Time in the Worship of God, in our publick or private Devotions. For commonly Men of Business are very much in Arrears with God upon this Account: In their active Age they had little Time to spare, or little Mind to spare it for the Uses of Religion; and therefore we may well retire some time before we die, to make up that Defect; and when we have done with the World, to give up ourselves wholly to the Service of God.

God. We should now be very importunate in our Prayers to God, that for the Merits and Intercession of Christ, he would freely pardon all the Sins, and Frailties, and Errors of our past Life; and give us such a comfortable Hope and Sense of his Love to us, as may support us in the Hour of Death, and sweeten the Terrors and Agonies of it. We should meditate on the great Love of God in sending Christ into the World to save Sinners; and contemplate the Heighth and Depth, and Length and Breadth of that Love of God, which passeth all human Understanding. We should represent to ourselves the wonderful Condescension of the Son of God in becoming Man; his amazing Goodness in dying for Sinners, the Just for the Unjust, to reconcile us to God. And when we have warmed our Souls with such Thoughts as these, we should break forth into Raptures and Extasies of Devotion, in the Praise of our Maker and Redeemer. *Worthy is the Lamb that was slain, to receive power, and riches, and wisdom, and strength, and honour, and glory, and blessing. Blessing, and honour, and glory, and power be unto him that sitteth on the throne, and to the Lamb for ever and ever.* Rev. v. 12, 13.

And besides other Reasons, which make this a very proper Preparation for Death, this accustoms us to the Work and Employment of the next World: For Heaven is a Life of Devotion and Praise; there we shall see God,

and

and admire and adore him, and sing eternal Hallelujahs to him. And therefore nothing can so dispose and prepare us for Heaven, as to have our Hearts ready turned to the Praises of God, ravished with Love, transported with his Glory and Perfections, and swallowed up in the most profound and humble Adorations of him.

3. Thus when we are going into another World, it becomes us most to have our Thoughts there; to consider what a blessed Place that is, where we shall be delivered from all the Fears, and Sorrows, and Temptations of this World; where we shall see God and the blessed Jesus, and converse with Angels and glorified Spirits, and live an endless Life without fear of dying: Where there is nothing but perfect Love and Peace; no cross Interests and Factions to contend with; no Storms to ruffle or discompose our Joy and Rest to Eternity: Where there is no Pain, no Sickness, no Labour; no Care to refresh the Weariness, or to repair the Decays of a mortal Body; not so much as the Image of Death to interrupt our constant Enjoyments. Where there is a perpetual Day, and an eternal Calm, where our Souls shall attain their utmost Perfection of Knowledge and Virtue. Where we shall serve God, not with dull, and sleepy, and unaffecting Devotions, but with piercing Thoughts, with Life and Vigour, with Ravishment and Transport. In a Word,

where there are such things, *as neither eye hath seen nor ear heard, neither hath it entered into the heart of man to conceive.*

These are proper Thoughts for a Man who is to compose himself for Death: Not to think of the pale and ghastly Looks of Death, when he shall be wrapp'd up in his Winding-Sheet: Not to think of the dark and melancholy Retirements of the Grave, where his Body must rot and putrify, till it be raised up again immortal and glorious: But to lift up his Eyes to Heaven to view that lightsome and happy Country; with *Moses* to ascend up into the Mount, to take a Prospect of the heavenly *Canaan*, whither he is going. This will conquer even the natural Aversions to Death, and make us, with St *Paul*, desirous to be dissolved, and to be with Christ, which is best of all; make it as easy to us to leave this World for Heaven, as it is to remove into a more pleasant and wholesome Air, or into a more convenient and beautiful House. So easy, so pleasant will it be to die with such Thoughts as these about us.

This indeed ought to be the constant Exercise of the Christian Life: It is fit for all Times and for all Persons; and without some Degree of it, it is impossible to conquer the Temptations of the World, or to live in the Practice of divine and heavenly Virtues. But this ought to be the constant Business, or Entertainment rather of those happy Men who

who have lived long enough in the World, to take a fair Leave of it; who have run through all the Scenes and Stages of human Life, and have now Death and another World in View and Prospect.

And it is this makes a Retirement from the World so necessary, or very useful; not merely to ease our bodily Labours, and to get a little Rest from Business, or dissolve in Sloth and Idleness, or to wander about to seek a Companion, or to hear News, or to talk Politicks, or to find out some way to spend Time, which now lies upon our Hands, and is more easy and troublesome to us than Business was. This is a more dangerous State, and does more indispose us for a happy Death, than all the Cares and Troubles of an active Life: But we must retire from this World, to have more Leisure and greater Opportunities to prepare for the next; to adorn and cultivate our Minds, and dress our Souls like a Bride, who is adorned to meet her Bridegroom.

When Men converse much in this World, and are distracted with the Cares and Business of it: When they live in a Crowd of Customers or Clients, and are hurried from their Shops to the *Exchange* or *Custom-House*, or from their Chambers to the Bar; and when they have discharged one Obligation, are pressed hard by another, that at Night they have hardly Spirits left to say their Prayers, nor any Time for them in the Morning; and the Lord's Day itself is thought more proper for Rest and Refreshment than Devotion: I say, what dull, cold Apprehensions must such Men have of another World? And after all the Care we can take, how will this World insinuate itself into our Affections, when it employs our Time and Thoughts; when our whole Business is buying and selling, and driving good Bargains, and making Conveyances and Settlements of Estates? How will this disorder our Passions, occasion Feuds and Quarrels, give us a Tincture of Pride, Ambition, Covetousness? That there is Work enough after a busy Life, even for very good Men to wash out these Stains and Pollutions, and to get the Taste and Relish of this World out of their Mouths, and to revive and quicken the Sense of God, and of another World.

This is a sufficient Reason for such Men, as I observ'd before, to think when it is Time to leave off, and if not wholly to withdraw from the World, yet to contract their Business, and to have the Command of it, that they may have more Leisure to take care of their Souls, before they have so near a Call and Summons to Death; but much more necessary is it, when Death is even at the Door, and by the Course of Nature we know that it is so.

It

It is very proper to leave the World, before we are removed out of it, that we may know how to live without it, that we may not carry any Hankerings after this World with us into the next; and therefore it is very fitting, that there should be a kind of middle State between this World and the next; that is, That we should withdraw from this World, and wean ourselves from it, even while we are in it; which will make it more easy to part with this World, and make us more fit to go to the next. But it seems strangely undecent, unless the Necessities of their Families, or the Necessities of the Publick call for it, and exact it, to see Men who are just a-going out of the World, who, it may be, bow as much under their Riches as under their Age, plunging themselves over Head and Ears in this World, courting new Honours and Preferments, with as much Zeal as those who are but entering into the World. It is to be fear'd, such Men think very little of another World, and will never be satisfy'd with Earth, 'till they are buried in it.

SECT. IV.

What Use to make of the Shortness of human Life.

II. AS the general Period of human Life is fix'd and determined by God, so this Term of Life, at the utmost Extent of it, it, is but very short. For what are threescore and ten, or fourscore Years? How soon do they pass away like a Dream; and when they are gone, How few and empty do they appear? The best way to be sensible of this, is not to look forward; for we fancy Time to come, to be much longer than we find it; but to look backward upon the Time which is past, and as long as we can remember; And how suddenly are thirty or forty Years gone? How little do we remember how they are past? But gone they are, and the rest are going apace, while we eat, and drink, and sleep; and when they are gone too, we shall be sensible, that all together was but very short. Now from hence I shall observe several things, of very great Use for the Government of our Lives.

1. If our Lives be so very short, it concerns us to lose none of our Time: For does it become us to be prodigal of our Time, when we have so little of it? We either ought to make as much of our Lives as we can, or not complain that they are short; for that is a greater Reproach to ourselves, than to the Order of Nature, and the Providence of God: For, it seems, we have more Time than we care to live in, more that we think necessary to improve to the true Ends and Purposes of living; and if we can spare so much of our Lives, it seems they are too long for us, how short soever they are in themselves. And
when

when our Lives are too long already for the Generality of Mankind to improve wisely, Why should God give us more Time to play with, and to squander away? And yet let us all reflect upon ourselves, and consider, how much of our Lives we have perfectly lost, how careless we have been of our Time, which is the most precious Thing in the World; how we have given it to every body that will take it, and given away so much of ourselves, and our own Being with it.

Should Men sit down, and take a Review of their Lives, and draw up a particular Account of the Expence of their Time, after they come to Years of Discretion and Understanding, what a shameful Bill would it be? What unreasonable Abatements of Life? How little Time would there be at the Foot of the Account, which might be called living?

So much extraordinary for eating, and drinking, and sleeping, beyond what the Support and Refreshment of Nature requir'd; so much in Courtship, Wantonness and Lust; so much in Drinking and Revelling; so much for the Recovery of the last Night's Debauch; so much in gaming and Masquerades; so much in paying and receiving formal and impertinent Visits, in idle and extravagant Discourses, in censuring and reviling our Neighbours or our Governors; so much in dressing and adorning our Bodies; so many blank and long Parentheses of Life, wasted in doing nothing, or in counting the slow and tedious Minutes, or chiding the Sun for making no more haste down, and delaying their Evening Assignations. But how little would there appear in most Mens Account, spent to the true Ends of living?

The very naming of these things is sufficient to convince any considering Man, that this is really a mispending of Time, and a flinging away great Part of a very short Life to no Purpose: But to make you all sensible of this, consider with me, when we may be said to lose our Time; for Time passes away very swiftly, and we can no more hold it, than we can stop the Chariot-Wheels of the Sun: But all Time that is past, is not lost; indeed no Time is our own, but what is past or present; and its being past makes it never the less our own, if ever it were so. But then we lose our Time,

1. When it turns to no account to us when it is gone; when we are never the better for it in Body or Soul. This is the true way of judging, by our own Sense and Feeling, whether we have spent our Time well or ill, by observing what Relish it leaves upon our Minds, and what the Effects of it are, when it is past: How vainly soever Men spend their Time, they find some Pleasure and Diversion, and Entertainment in it, while it lasts, but the next Morning it is all vanished,

as

as their Night Dreams are; and if they are not the worse for it, they find themselves never the better. And this is a certain Sign, that our Time was vainly and foolishly spent; that when it is gone, it can be brought into no Account of our Lives, but that of idle Expences. Whatever is good, whatever is in any Degree useful, leaves some Satisfaction when it is gone; and Time so spent, we can place to our Account, and all such Time is not lost: But Men who spend one Day after another, in Mirth and Jollity, and Entertainments, in Visits, or Gaming, &c. can give no other Account of it, but that it is a pleasant Way of spending Time. And that it is the true Name for it, not living, but spending Time, which they know not how otherwise to pass away; when their Time is spent, they have all they intended, and their Enjoyments pass away with their Time, and there is an End of both; and it were somewhat more tolerable, if they themselves could end with their Time too. But when Men must out-live Time, and the Effects of Time must last to Eternity, that Time, which if it have no ill, yet has no good Effects more lasting than itself, is utterly lost.

2*dly*, To be sure that Time is doubly lost, which we cannot review without Amazement and Horror; I mean, in which we have contracted some great Guilt, which we have not only spent vainly, but wickedly, which we

ourselves

ourselves with had never been, which we desire to forget, and could be glad that both God and Men could forget it too. For is not that lost Time, which loses us, which undoes us, which distracts us with guilty Fears, which we would give all the World we could lose out of the Account of our Lives, and could lose the very Remembrance of it? I think that somewhat worse than lost Time, which forfeits a blessed Eternity, and for which Men must lose their Souls for ever.

3*dly*, That is lost Time too, which Men must live over again, and tread back their Steps like him who has mistaken his Way: Not that we can re-call our past Time, and those Minutes that are fled from us; but we must substitute some of our remaining Time in its room, and begin our Lives again, and undo what we have formerly done. This is the Case of those who have spent great Part of their Lives ill, whenever they are convinced of their Folly and Danger; they must give all their past Lives for lost; and it may be when half, or two thirds, or more of their Lives are spent, they must then begin to live, and to undo by Repentance and Reformation, the Errors and Follies, and Impieties of their former Lives. Now I suppose all Men will confess that Time to be lost, which they must unlive again; to be sure Penitents are very sensible it is; and I wish all those would consider it, who resolve to spend their youthful
and

and vigorous Age in Sin, and to repent hereafter; that is, they resolve to fling away the greatest and best Part of their Lives, and to begin to live when they see themselves a dying: This, I am sure, is no Remedy against a short Life, to resolve not to live one third of it.

2*dly*, Since our Life is so very short, it becomes us to live as much as we can in so short a Time; for we must not measure the Length or Shortness of our Lives by Days, or Months, or Years, that is the Measure of our Duration or Being; but to live and to be are two Things, and of a distinct Consideration and Account.

To live, when we speak of a Man, signifies to act like a reasonable Creature, to exercise his Understanding and Will upon such Objects as answer the Dignity and Perfection of human Nature, to be employed in such Actions as are proper to his Nature, and distinguish a Man from all other Creatures. And therefore, though a Man must eat and drink, and perform the other Offices of a natural Life, which are common to him with Beasts; yet this is not to live like a Man, any otherwise than as these common Actions are govern'd by Reason and Rules of Virtue; but he who minds nothing higher than this, lives like a Beast, not like a Man. A Life of Reason, Religion, and Virtue, is properly the Life of a Man; because it is peculiar to him, and

distinguishes

distinguishes him from all other Creatures in this World: And therefore he who improves his Knowledge and Understanding most; who has his Passions and Appetites under the best Government; who does most good, and makes himself most useful to the World; though he does not continue longer, yet he lives more and longer than other Men; that is, he exerts more frequent and more perfect Acts of a rational Life.

But besides this, this Life is only in order to a better Life: It is not for itself, but only a Passage to, and a State of Trial and Probation for, Immortality; and it were hardly worth the while to come into the World upon any meaner Design. And therefore he lives most, who improves the Grace of God to make himself most fit for Heaven, and qualified for the greatest Rewards, for the richest and the brightest Crowns; who knows God most, and worships him in the most perfect Manner, with the greatest Ravishments and Transports of Spirit; who lives most above this World in the Exercise of the most divine Virtues; who does most Service to God in the World, and improves all his Talents to the best Advantage: In a word, who most adorns and perfects his own Mind, brings most Glory to God, and does most good to Men. Such a Man at thirty Years old has lived more, nay, indeed may properly be said to have lived longer, than any old decrepid Sinner; for he has

has not lived at all to the Purposes of Man, or to the Ends of the other World. That Man has lived a great while, how short soever the Time be, who is old enough for Heaven, and for Eternity; who has laid up Riches and glorious Treasures for himself in the other World; who has answered the Ends of his Life, and is fit to remove out of it. This is the true Way of measuring our Lives by Acts of Piety and Virtue, by our Improvements in Knowledge and Grace, and Wisdom, by our Ripeness for another World. And therefore, if we would live a great while in this World, we must, 1. Begin to live betimes. 2. We must have a care of all Interruptions and Intermissions of Life. 3. We must live apace.

1. We must begin to live betimes; that is, we must begin betimes to live like Men, and like Christians, to live to God, and to another World; that is, in a word, to be good betimes: For those who begin to live with the first Bloomings of Reason and Understanding, and give early and useful Specimens of Piety and Virtue, if they reach to old Age, they live three times as long as those who count indeed as many Years as they do, but, it may be, have not lived a third of their Time, but have lost it in Sin and Folly. The first can look back to the very Beginning of this Life, and enjoy all his past Years still, review them with Pleasure and Satisfaction,

Satisfaction, and bring them all to Account. But a late Penitent must date his Life from his Repentance and Reformation: He dares look no further back; for all beyond is lost, or worse than lost. It is like looking back upon the rude Chaos, which was nothing but Confusion and Darkness before God formed the World. Such is the Life of a Sinner before this new Birth, and new Creation: And therefore he has but a very little way to look back; can give but a very short Account of his Life; has but a very few Years of his Life which he dares own, and carry into the other World with him.

2. We must have a Care of all Interruptions and Intermissions of Life; that is, of falling back into Sin again, after some hopeful Beginnings. This is too often seen, that those, who by the Care and good Government, and wise Instructions of Parents and Tutors, have had the Principles of Virtue and Piety early instilled into them, and have had a good Relish of it themselves; yet when they have got loose from these Restraints, and fall into ill Company, and into the Way of Temptations, have a mind to try another Kind of Life, and to taste those Pleasures which they see Mankind so fond of; and too often try so long, 'till they grow as great Strangers to Piety and Virtue, as they were ignorant of Vice before. Now if such Men ever be reclaimed again, yet all their early
Beginnings

Beginnings of Life are loſt; for here is a long Interruption and Intermiſſion of Life, which ſets them back in the Account of Eternity. And thus it is proportionably in every wilful Sin we commit: It makes a Break in our Lives; does not only ſtop our Progreſs for a while, but ſets us backward. But he who begins betimes to live, without any, or very few, and very ſhort Interruptions, will be able to reckon a very long Life, by that time he attains to the common Period of human Life.

3. Eſpecially if we live apace. There is a living apace, as ſome call it; not to lengthen, but to ſhorten Life: When Men, by minding their Buſineſs well, can in ten or twenty Years deſtroy ſuch a Conſtitution of Body, and exhauſt that vital Heat and Vigour, which would have laſted another Man ſixty or eighty Years. This is to live much in a little Time, and to make an end of their Lives quickly; and the living apace, I mean, is to live much alſo in a little Time, but to double and treble our Lives, not to ſhorten them: That is, to do all the Good that ever we can; for the more Good we do, the more we live. Life is not mere Duration, but Action: Time is not Life, but we live, that is, we act in Time: And he who does two Days Work in one, lives as much in one Day, as other Men do in two. He who in one Year does as much improve his Mind in Knowledge and Wiſdom

dom, and all Christian Graces and Virtues; worships God as much and more devoutly, does as much Good to the World in all Capacities and Relations of Life, as another Man does in two, or three, or four: He lives so much proportionably longer than those other Men: He does the Work of so much Time, and this is equivalent to, nay, much better than, living so much Time. For he who can have the Reward of two hundred Years in the next World, and not live above threescore or fourscore here, I take to be a much happier Man, than he who spends two hundred Years in this World. This is the best Way of lengthening our Lives, by living doubly and trebly; which will make a vast Addition to our Lives in fifty or sixty Years: And then there will be no Reason to complain of the Shortness of them.

3*dly*, If our Lives are so very short, as most Men complain they are, surely we have little Reason to complain of spending the whole of these short Lives in the Service of God for an eternal Reward. What are threescore or fourscore Years, when compared to an Eternity? And therefore, setting aside all the present Advantages and Pleasures of a Life of Religion, that this is only to live, to improve and perfect our own Natures, serve God, and to do good in the World; suppose there were nothing in Religion but Hardships and Difficulties, a perpetual Force and Violence to Nature, a
constant

constant War with the World and the Flesh; cannot we endure all this so short a Time for an endless Reward? Men think their Days-work very well spent, when they receive their Wages at Night; and can go home and sup chearfully with their Family, and sleep sweetly as labouring Men use to do, all Night: And yet our Saviour compares all the Work and Industry of our Lives to Day-Labourers, in the Parable of the Houshoulder, who at several Hours of the Day hir'd Labourers to work in his Vineyard, and paid them their Wages at Night, *Matth.* xx. 1, *&c.*

We all confess, that threescore and ten years, if we live so long, is but a very short Time in itself, and quickly passes away: I am sure we all think so, when it is gone: And yet conider, how much of this Time is cut off by Infancy, Childhood, and Youth; while we are under the Care and Conduct of Parents and Governors, and are not our own Men. How much is spent in Sleeping, in Eating and Drinking, and necessary Diversions, for the Support and Repair of these mortal Bodies; in our necessary Business to provide for our Families, or to serve the Publick; which God allows and requires of us, and accounts it serving himself: While we live like Men, are sober and temperate, and just and faithful to our Trust, which we should do for our own sakes, and which all well-governed Societies require of us, without any Consideration of

L another

another World. So that there is but very little of this very short Life spent purely in the Service of God, and in the Care of our Souls, and the Concernments of a future State: And this is too much for an Eternity of Bliss and Happiness? To complain of Sobriety and Temperance, and moral Honesty, as such insufferable Burdens, that a Man had better be damn'd than submit to them, is not so much to complain of the Laws of God, as of all the wise Governments in the World, even in the Heathen World, which branded all these Vices with Infamy, and restrained and corrected them with condign Punishments: It is to complain of human Nature, which has made all these Vices infamous; and to think it better to be damned than to live like Men. And yet above two Thirds of our Time require the Exercise of few other Virtues but these: And whatever Difficulties Men may imagine in other Acts of Religion, if they can possibly think it so intolerable to love the greatest and the best Being; to praise and adore him, to whom we owe ourselves and all we have; to ask the Supply of our Wants from him who will be sure to give, if we faithfully ask; to raise our Hearts above this World, which is a Scene of Vanity, Emptiness, or Misery; and to delight ourselves in the Hope and Expectations of great and eternal Happiness, wherein the very Life of Religion consists: I say, if these be such very difficult

cult and uneaſy Things, (which one would
…der how they came to be difficult, or why
… ſhould be thought ſo) yet they employ
… little of our Time; and methinks a
… might bear it, to be happy for ever. I
ſure, Men take a great deal more Pains for
 World than Heaven would coſt them;
 when they have it, don't live to enjoy it.
… if this be thought worth their while,
…ly to ſpend a ſhort Life in the Service of
…, to obtain an endleſs and eternal Happi-
… is the beſt and moſt advantageous ſpend-
… our Time. And we muſt have a very
…n Opinion of Heaven and eternal Happi-
…, if we think it not worth the Obedience
… Service of a few Years, how difficult ſo-
r that were.

…*thly*, If our Lives are ſo very ſhort at their
…oſt Extent, the ſinful Pleaſures of this
…rld can be no great Temptation, when
…pared with an Eternity of Happineſs or
…ſery. Thoſe ſenſual Pleaſures which Men
… ſo fond of, and for the ſake of which they
…ak the Laws of God, and provoke his Ju-
…e, forfeit immortal Life, and expoſe them-
…es to all the Miſeries and Sufferings of an
…rnal Death, can laſt no longer than we live
…his World: And how little a while is that?
…hen we put off theſe Bodies, all bodily
…aſures periſh with them; nay indeed, as
… Bodies die and decay by Degrees, before
…y tumble into the Grave, ſo do our Plea-

sures sensibly decay too. As short as our Lives are, Men may outlive some of their most beloved Vices; and therefore, how luscious soever they may be, such short and dying Pleasures ought not to come in Competition with eternal Happiness or Misery. Whatever Things are in their own Nature, the Value of them increases or diminishes, according to the Length or Shortness of their Enjoyment. That which will last our Lives, and make them easy and comfortable, is to be preferred by wise Men before the most ravishing Enjoyments of a Day. And a Happiness which will out-last our Lives, and reach to Eternity, is to be preferred before the perishing Enjoyments of a short Life. Unless Men can think it better to be happy for threescore Years, than for ever; nay, unless Men think the Enjoyments of threescore Years a sufficient Recompence for eternal Want and Misery.

5*thly*, The Shortness of our Lives are a sufficient Answer to all those Arguments against Providence, taken from the Prosperity of bad Men, and the Miseries and Afflictions of the good; for both of them are so short, that they are nothing in the Account of Eternity. Were this Life to be consider'd by itself, without any Relation to a future State, the Difficulty would be greater, but not very great: Because a short Happiness, or a short Misery, chequer'd and intermix'd as all the Happiness and Miseries of this Life are,

are, is not very confiderable; nor were it worth the while either to make Objections againſt Providence, or to anſwer them, if Death put an End to us.

Bad Men who make theſe Objections againſt Providence, are very well contented to take the World as they find it, ſo they may have it without a Providence; which is a Sign that it is not their Diſlike of this World (though many times they ſuffer as much in it as good Men do) which makes them quarrel at Providence, but the Dread and Fear of another World. And this proves that they think this World a very tolerable Place, whether there be a Providence or not. And if ſo ſhort a Life as this is be but tolerable, it is a ſufficient Juſtification of Providence, that this Life is well enough for its Continuance; a very mixt and imperfect State indeed, but very ſhort too: Such a State as bad Men themſelves would like very well without another Life after it; and ſuch a State as good Men like very well with another Life to follow. It is not a Spite at human Life which makes them reject a Providence; as any one would gueſs, who hears them object their own Proſperity, and the Calamities of good Men, as Arguments againſt Providence; both which they like very well. And whatever there may be in theſe Objections, ſuppoſing there were no other Life after this, yet when they all vaniſh at the very naming of another

Life,

Life, where good Men will be rewarded, and the wicked punished; it is ridiculous to prove, that there is no other Life after this, becaufe Rewards and Punifhments are not difpenfed with that exact Juftice in this Life, as we might fuppofe God would obferve, if there were no other Life. To prove that there is no other Life after this, becaufe good and bad Men do not receive their juft Rewards in this Life, is an Argument which becomes the Wit and Underftanding of an Atheift: For they muft firft take it for granted, that there is no Providence, before this Argument can prove any thing. For if there be a Providence, then the Profperity of bad Men, and the Sufferings of the good, is a much better Argument that there is another Life after this, where Rewards and Punifhments fhall be more equally diftributed. Thus, when they difpute againft Providence, from the Profperity of bad Men, and the Calamities of the good; before this can prove any thing, they muft take it for granted, that there is no other Life after this, where good Men fhall be rewarded, and the wicked punifhed: For if there be, it is eafy enough to juftify the Providence of God, as to the prefent Profperity of bad Men, and the Sufferings of the good. So that they muft of Neceffity difpute in a Circle, as the Papifts do between the Church and the Scriptures, when they either prove that there is no Providence, or no Life

after

after this from the unequal Rewards and Punishments of good and bad Men in this World. For, in effect, they prove that there is no Providence, because there is no Life after this; or that there is no Life after this, because there is no Providence. For the Prosperity of bad Men, and the Sufferings of the good, proves neither of them, unless you take the other for granted. And if you will prove them both by this Medium, you must take them both for granted by turns; and that is the easier and safer Way to take them for granted, without exposing themselves to the Scorn of wise Men by such kind of Proofs. But yet though this were no Objection against the Being of another World, and a Providence; yet had the Prosperity of bad Men, and the Calamities of the good continued some hundred Years, it had been a greater Difficulty, and a greater Temptation than now it is. The Prosperity of the Wicked is a much less Objection when it is so easily answered, as the Psalmist does, *Yet a little while, and the wicked shall not be; yea, thou shalt diligently consider this place, and it shall not be*, Psal. xxxvii. 10. When the very same Persons who have been the Spectators and Witnesses of his prosperous Villanies, live to see a quick and sudden End of him: *I have seen the wicked in great power, and spreading himself like a green bay-tree; yet he passed away, and lo he was not; yea, I sought him, but he could not be found,* 35, 36. And this is enough also to support the Spirits of good Men: *For this cause we faint not; but though our outward man perish, yet the inward man is renewed day by day. For our light affliction, which is but for a moment, worketh for us a far more exceeding and eternal weight of glory,* 2 Cor. iv. 16, 17.

SECT. V.

The Time, and Manner, and Circumstances of every particular Man's Death, is not determined by an absolute and unconditional Decree.

II. Though GOD, who knows all Things, does know also the Time, and Manner, and Circumstances of every particular Man's Death, yet it does not appear that he has by any absolute and unconditional Decree, fix'd and determined the particular Time of every Man's Death. This is that famous Question which *Beverovicius,* a learned Physician, was so much concerned to have resolved, and consulted so many learned Men about it, as supposing it would be a great Injury to his Profession, did Men believe that the Time of their Death was so absolutely determined by God, that they could neither die sooner, nor live longer than that fatal Period, whether they took the Advice and

and Prescriptions of the Physicians or not. But this was a vain Fear; for there are some Speculations which Men never live by, how vehemently soever they contend for them: A Sceptick who pretends that there is nothing certain, and will dispute with you as long as you please about it, yet will not venture his own Arguments so far as to leap into Fire and Water, nor to stand before the Mouth of a loaded Cannon, when you give Fire to it. Thus Men who talk most about fatal Necessity, and absolute Decrees, yet they will eat and drink to preserve themselves in Health, and take Physick when they are sick, and as heartily repent of their Sins, and vow Amendment and Reformation, when they think themselves a dying, as if they did not believe one Word of such absolute Decrees, and fatal Necessity, as they talk of at other Times.

I do not intend to engage in this Dispute of Necessity and Fate, of Prescience and absolute Decrees, which will be Disputes as long as the World lasts, unless Men grow wiser than to trouble themselves with such Questions as are above their Reach, and which they can never have a clear Notion and Perception of; but all that I intend to shew you, according to the Scripture-Account of it, That the Period of our Lives is not so peremptorily determined by God, but that we may lengthen or shorten them, live longer, or die

sooner

sooner, according as we behave ourselves in this World.

Now this is very plain from all those Places of Scripture, where God promises long Life to good Men, and threatens to shorten the Lives of the Wicked, *Psal.* xci. 16. *With long life will I satisfy him, and shew him my salvation.* *Solomon* tells us of Wisdom, *Length of days is in her right hand, and in her left riches and honour,* Prov. iii. 16. *The fear of the Lord prolongeth days, but the years of the wicked shall be shortened,* Prov. x. 27. Thus God has promised long Life to those who honour their Parents, in the fifth Commandment; and the same Promise is made in more general Terms to those who observe the Statutes and Commandments of God, *Deut.* iv. 40. Upon the same Condition God promised long Life to King *Solomon,* 1 *Kings* iii. 14. *And if thou wilt walk in my ways, to keep my statutes and commandments, as thy father David did walk, then will I lengthen thy days.* The same is supposed in *David's* Prayer to God, *not to take him away in the midst of his days,* Psal. cii. 24. And in *Psal.* lv. 23. he tells us, That *bloody and deceitful men shall not live out half their days.* Now one would reasonably conclude from hence, that God has not absolutely and unconditionally determined the fatal Period of every Man's Life, because he has conditionally promised to prolong Mens Lives, or threaten'd to shorten them;

them; for what Place can there be for conditional Promises, where an absolute Decree is past? How can any Man be said not to live out half his Days, if he lives as long as God has decreed he shall live? For if the Period of every particular Man's Life be determined by God, none are his Days but what God has decreed for him.

As for Matter of Fact, it is plain and evident, both that Men shorten their own Lives, and that God shortens them for them, and that in such a Manner as will not admit of an absolute and unconditional Decree: Thus some Men destroy a healthful and vigorous Constitution of Body by Intemperance and Lust; and do as manifestly kill themselves, as those who hang, or poison, or drown themselves; and both these Sorts of Men, I suppose, may be said to shorten their own Lives; and so do those who rob, or murther, or commit any other Villainy, which forfeits their Lives to publick Justice; or quarrel and fall in a Duel, and the like: And yet you will no more say, that God decreed and determined the Death of these Men, than he did their Sin.

Thus God himself very often shortens the Lives of Men, by Plague and Famine, and Sword, and such other Judgments as he executes upon a wicked World: And this must be confess'd to be the Effect of God's Counsel and Decrees, as a Judge decrees and pronounces

ces the Death of a Malefactor; but this is not an absolute and unconditional Decree, but is occasioned by their Sins and Provocations, as all Judgments are: They might have lived longer, and escaped these Judgments, had they been virtuous, and obedient to God; for if they should have lived no longer, whether they had sinned or not, their Death, by what Judgments soever they are cut off, is not so properly the Execution of Justice, as of a peremptory Decree; their Lives are not shortened, but their fatal Period is come.

Indeed unless we make the Providence of God, not the Government of a wise and free Agent, who acts *pro re nata*, and rewards and punishes as Men deserve, as the Scripture represents it; but an unavoidable Execution of a long Series of fatal and necessary Events, from the Beginning to the End of the World, as the Stoicks thought; we must acknowledge, that in the Government of free Agents, God has reserved to himself a free Liberty of lengthening or shortening Mens Lives, as will best serve the Ends of Providence. For if we will allow Man to be a free Agent, and that he is not under a Necessity of sinning, and deserving to be cut off at such a Time, or in such a Manner, the Application of Rewards and Punishments to him must be free also, or else they may be ill applied: He may be punished when he deserves to be rewarded; the fatal Period of Life may
fall

fall out at such a Time, when he most of all deserves long Life, and when the lengthening his Life would be a publick Blessing to the World. Fatal and necessary Events can never be fitted to the Government of free Agents, no more than you can make a Clock, which shall strike exactly for Time and Number, when such a Man speaks, let him speak when, or name what Number he pleases: And yet there is nothing of greater Moment in the Government of the World, than a free Power and Liberty of lengthening or shortening Mens Lives: For nothing more overawes Mankind, and keeps them more in dependance on God; nothing gives a more signal Demonstration of a divine Power, or Vengeance, or Protection; nothing is a greater Blessing to Families or Kingdoms, or a greater Punishment to them, than the Life or Death of a Parent, of a Child, of a Prince; and therefore it is as necessary to reserve this Power to God, as to assert a Providence. There are two or three Places of Scripture, which are urged in Favour of the contrary Opinion. *Job* xiv. 5. *Seeing his days are determined, the number of his months are with thee; thou hast appointed his bounds that he cannot pass.* Job vii. 1. *Is there not an appointed time to man upon earth? Are not his days also like the days of an hireling?* Which refer not to the particular Period of every Man's Life, but, as I observ'd before, to the general Period of human Life,

Life, which is fix'd and determin'd, which is therefore called the Days or the Years of Man, becaufe God hath appointed this the ordinary Time of Man's Life; as when God threatens that the wicked fhall not live out half their Days; that is, half that Time which is allotted for Men to live on Earth: For they have no other Intereft in thefe Days, but that they are the Days of Man, and therefore might be their Days too.

From what I have now difcourfed, there are two Things very plainly to be obferved: 1. That Men may contribute very much to the lengthening or fhortening their own Lives. 2. That the Providence of God does peculiarly over-rule and determine this Matter.

1. As for the firft, there is no need to prove it; for we fee Men deftroy their own Lives every Day, either by Intemperance and Luft, or more open Violence, by forfeiting their Lives to publick Juftice, or by provoking the divine Vengeance: And therefore whoever defires a long Life, to fill up the Number of his Days, which God hath allotted us in this World, muft keep himfelf from fuch deftructive Vices, muft practife the moft healthful Virtues, muft make God his Friend, and engage his Providence for his Defence. Can any Thing be more abfurd, than to hear Men promife themfelves long Life, and reckon upon forty or fifty Years to come, when they run into thofe Excefses, which will make

a quick

a quick and speedy End of them? Which will either inflame or corrupt their Blood, and let a Fever or a Dropsy into their Veins, or bring Rottenness into their Bones, or engage them in some fatal Quarrel, or ruin their Estates, and send them to seek their Fortune upon the Road, which commonly brings them to the Gallows? What a fatal Cheat is this, which Men put upon themselves; especially when they sin in Hope of Time to repent, and commit such Sins as will give them no Time to repent in?

The Advice of the *Psalmist* is much better: *What man is he that desireth life, and loveth many days, that he may see good? Keep thy tongue from evil, and thy lips from speaking guile: depart from evil, and do good; seek peace, and pursue it.* These are natural and moral Causes of a long Life: But that is not all, *For the eyes of the Lord are upon the righteous, and his ears are open unto their cry; the face of the Lord is against them that do evil, to cut off the remembrance of them from the earth.* That is, God will prolong the Lives of good Men, and cut off the Wicked; not that this is a general Rule without Exception; but it is the ordinary Method of Providence, *Psal.* xxxiv. 12, 13, &c.

2. For though God has not determined how long every Man shall live, by an absolute and unconditional Decree; yet if a Sparrow does not fall to the Ground without our Father, much

much less does Man. No Man can go out of this World, no more than he can come into it, but by a special Providence; no Man can destroy himself, but by God's Leave; no Disease can kill, but when God pleases; no mortal Accident can befal us, but by God's Appointment; who is therefore said to deliver the Man into the Hands of his Neighbour, who is killed by an evil Accident, *Deut.* xix. 4, 5. Those wasting Judgments of Plague and Pestilence, Famine and Sword, are appointed by God, and have their particular Commissions where to strike; as we may see, *Lev.* xxvi. 47. *Jer.* vi. 7. *Isa.* lxv. 12. *Jer.* xv. 2. *Psal.* cxi. and several other Places. All the Rage and Fury of Men cannot take away our Lives, but by God's particular Permission, *Matt.* x. 28, 29, 30, 31.

And this lays as great an Obligation on us, as the Love of Life can, which is the dearest Thing in this World, to serve and please God; this will make us secure from all Fears and Dangers. *My times,* saith *David, are in thy hand; deliver me from the hand of mine enemies, and from them that persecute me,* Psal. xxxi. 15. This encourages us to pray to God, for ourselves, or our Friends, whatever Danger our Lives are in, either from Sickness, or from Men. There is no Case wherein he can't help us; when he sees fit, he can rectify the Disorders of Nature, and correct an ill Habit of Body, and rebuke the most raging

raging Distempers, which mock at all the Arts of Physick, and Powers of Drugs, and many times does so by insensible Methods. To conclude: This is a great Satisfaction to good Men, that our Lives are in the Hands of God; that though there be not such a fix'd and immoveable Period set to them, yet Death cannot come but by God's Appointment.

SECT. VI.

The particular Time when we are to die, is unknown and uncertain to us.

III. THE particular Time when any of us are to die, is unknown and uncertain to us; and this is that which we properly call the Uncertainty of our Lives; that we know not when we shall die, whether this Night or To-morrow, or twenty Years hence. There is no need to prove this, but only to mind you of it, and to acquaint you what wise Use you are to make of it.

1. This shews how unreasonable it is to flatter ourselves with the Hope of long Life; I mean, of prolonging our Lives near the utmost Term and Period of human Life, which tho' it be but short in itself, is yet the longest that any Man can hope to live. No wise Man will promise himself that which he can have no Reason to expect, but what has very

often

often failed others: For let us seriously consider, what Reason any of us have to expect a long Life. Is it because we are young, and healthful, and vigorous? And do we not daily see young Men die? Can Youth, or Beauty, or Strength, secure us from the Arrests of Death? Is it because we see some Men live to a great Age? But this was no Security to those who died young, and left a great many Men behind them, who had lived twice or thrice their Age; and therefore we may also see a great many old Men, and die young ourselves. It is possible we may live to old Age, because some do; but it is more likely we shall not, because there are more that die young. The Truth is, the Time of dying is so uncertain, the Ways of dying so infinite, so unseen, so casual and fortuitous to us, that instead of promising ourselves long Life, no wise Man will promise himself a Week, nor venture any thing of great Moment and Consequence upon it. The Hope of long Life is nothing else but Self-flattery: The Fondness Men have for Life, and that Partiality they have for themselves, persuades them, that they shall live as long as any Man can live, and shall escape those Diseases and fatal Accidents with which our Bills of Mortality are fill'd every Week: But then you should consider, that other Men are as dear to themselves, as you are, and flatter themselves as much with long Life, as you do;

but

but their Hopes very often deceive them, and so may your's.

But you'll say, To what Purpose is all this? Why so much Pains to put us out of Conceit with the Hopes of living long? For what Hurt is it, if we do flatter ourselves a little more in this Matter than we have Reason for? If it should prove only a deceitful Dream, yet it makes Life chearful and comfortable, and gives us a true Relish of it; and why should we disturb ourselves, and make Life uneasy, by the perpetual Thoughts of dying?

Now I confess, were there no Hurt and Danger in it, this were as ill-natur'd and spiteful a Thing as could be done; and the least Recompence I could make, would be to ask you pardon for it, and leave you to enjoy the Comforts of Life securely for the future; to live as long as you can, and let Death come when it will, without being looked for: But I apprehend a great deal of Danger in such deceitful and flattering Hopes; and that is the Reason why I dissuade you from it. For,

1. The Hope of long Life is apt to make us fond of this World, which is as great a Mischief to us, as to expose us to all the Temptations and Flatteries of it. That we must die and leave this World, is a good Reason indeed why we ought not to be fond of it; why we should live like Pilgrims and

Strangers here, as I obferv'd before: But few Men, who hope to live threefcore or fourfcore Years, think much of this; tho' it be comparatively fhort in refpect of Eternity, yet it is a great while to live, and a great while to enjoy this World in; and that is thought a very valuable Happinefs, which can be enjoyed fo long. And then Men let loofe their Defires and Affections, endeavour to get as much of this World as they can; and to enjoy as much of it as they can; and not only to tafte, but to take full and plentiful Draughts of the intoxicating Pleafures of it. And how dangerous this is, I need not tell any Man, who confiders, that all the Wickednefs of Mankind is owing to too great a Fondnefs and Paffion for this World.

And therefore, if we would live like Pilgrims, and fit loofe from all the Enjoyments of this World; we muft remember, that our Stay is uncertain here, that we have no Leafe of our Lives, but may be turned out of our earthly Tenements at Pleafure. For what Man would be fond of laying up great Treafures on Earth, who remembers, *That this night his foul may be taken from him; and then whofe fhall all thefe things be?* What Man would place his Happinefs in fuch Enjoyments, which, for ought he knows, he may be taken from To-morrow? Thefe are indeed melancholy and mortifying Confiderations, and that is the true Ufe of them, for it is necef-

fary

sary we should be mortified to this World; to cure the Love of it, and conquer its Temptations: *For if any man love the world, the love of the Father is not in him: For all that is in the world, the lusts of the flesh, the lusts of the eye, and the pride of life, is not of the Father, but of the world.*

2. As the Hopes of long Life give great Advantage to the Temptations of this World, so they weaken the Hopes and Fears of the other World; they strengthen our Temptations, and weaken us, which must needs be of very fatal Consequence to us in our spiritual Warfare. All that we have to oppose against the flattering Temptations of this World, are the Hopes and Fears of the World to come; but the Hope of long Life sets the next World at too great a Distance to conquer this: What is present works more powerfully upon our Minds than what is absent; and the farther any thing is off, the less powerful it is.

To make you sensible of this, I shall only desire you to remember, what Thoughts you have had of another World, when the present Fears of Dying have given you a nearer View of it. Good Lord! What Agonies have I seen dying Sinners in? How penitent, how devout, how resolved upon a new Course of Life; which too often vanish like a Dream, when the Fear of Death is over. What is the Reason of this Difference? Heaven and

Hell is the very fame when we are in Health, as when we are fick; and I will fuppofe that you do as firmly believe a Heaven and Hell in Health, as in Sicknefs. The only thing then that makes the Thoughts of the other World fo ftrong, and powerful, and affecting when we are fick, is, that we fee the other World near us, that we are juft a ftepping into it, and this makes it our prefent Concernment; but in Health we fee the other World a great way off, and therefore do not think it of fuch near and prefent Concernment: And what we do not think ourfelves at prefent concern'd in, or not much concern'd in, how great and valuable foever it be in itfelf, will either not affect us at all, or very little. Thus, while bad Men place the other World at a great Diftance from them, and out of Sight, they have no Reftraint at all upon their Lufts and Paffions; and good Men themfelves, at the greater Diftance they fee the other World, are fo much the lefs affected by it; which damps their Zeal and their Devotion, and makes them lefs active and vigorous in doing Good.

And there is fo much the more Danger in this, becaufe Men look upon the other World as fartheft off, and fo are leaft concerned about it, when the Thoughts of the other World are moft ufeful and moft neceffary to them. In the Heat and Vigour of Youth, Men are moft expos'd to the Temptations of Flefh
and

and Senſe, and have moſt need to think of another World, and a future Judgment: But thoſe who promiſe themſelves a long Life, ſee Death and another World ſo far off, while they are young, that it moves them as little, as if there were no other World.

And though one would think, that as our Lives waſte, and the other World grows near, ſo we ſhould recover a more lively Senſe of it; yet we find it quite otherwiſe: When Men have been us'd to think the next World a great way off, they will never think it near till it comes; and when they have been us'd to think of the other World without any Paſſion or Concernment for it, it is almoſt an impoſſible thing to give any Quickneſs and Paſſion to ſuch Thoughts: For when any Thoughts, and the Paſſion that properly belongs to ſuch Thoughts, have been a great while ſeparated, it is a hard thing to unite them again; to begin to think of that with Paſſion and Concern, which we have been uſed for thirty or forty Years to think of without any Concernment.

3. Another dangerous Effect of flattering ourſelves with long Life, is, that it encourages Men to ſin with the vain Hopes and Reſolutions of repenting before they die. When Men are convinced, that if they live and die in Sin, they muſt be miſerable for ever; as I believe moſt profeſſed Chriſtians are, as I am ſure all muſt be, who believe the Goſpel of

our Saviour; there is no other possible Way to ward off this Blow, and to sin securely under such Convictions, but by resolving to repent, and to make their Peace with God before they die: They flatter themselves they have a great while yet to live, Judgment is a great way off, and therefore they may indulge themselves a while, and enjoy the Sweets of Sin, and gratify their youthful Inclinations, and learn the Vanity of the World by Experience, as their Forefathers have done before them; and then they will grow as wise and grave, and declaim against the Follies and Vanities of Youth, and be as penitent, and as devout and religious, as any of them all.

Whoever considers the Uncertainty of human Life, if he should hear Men talk at this rate, would either conclude that they were mad, or merrily disposed; but could never guess that they were in their Wits, and in good earnest too; but if we will allow Men to be in their Wits, who can promise themselves long Life, when they see every Day, how uncertain Life is; (and if we will not allow such Men to be in their Wits, above two thirds of the World are mad) this gives a plain Account how Men may resolve to sin while they are young, and to repent when they are old: For it is only the flattering Hopes of a long Life, that can encourage Men in a Course of Sin: Men indeed, who do not promise themselves long Life, may commit

commit a particular Sin, and refolve to repent of it as foon as they have done, which are a more modeft Sort of Sinners, of which more prefently; but I fpeak now of thofe (and too many fuch there are) who refolve to take their Fill of this World, while Youth, and Strength, and Health laft, and to grow fober and religious when they grow old; the Confequence of which is, that they refolve to be damned, unlefs they live till they are old, or till they grow weary of their Sins, and learn more Wifdom by Age and Experience.

Now I fhall not infift at prefent upon the Hazard fuch Men run, of not living till the Time comes which they have allotted for their Repentance, which belongs to another Argument; but only what a dangerous Thing it is to be tempted to a Cuftom and Habit of Sinning, by the Hope of long Life, and of Time enough to repent in; for there is not a greater Cheat in the World, that Men put upon themfelves, than to indulge themfelves in all Manner of Wickedneffes, to contract ftrong and powerful Habits of Vice, with a Refolution to repent of their Sins, and to forfake them before they die.

The Experience of the World fufficiently proves how vain this is; for though fome fuch Men may live while they are old, how feldom is it feen that they repent of their youthful Debaucheries when they grow old? They ftill retain their Love and Affection for thofe Sins,

Sins, which they can commit no longer; and repent of nothing, but that they are grown old, and cannot be so wicked as they were when they were young.

And is there any Reason in the World to expect it should be otherwise? Do we not know what the Power of Habit and Custom is? How the Love of Sin increases with the repeated Commission of it? And is the spending our youthful Strength and Vigour in Sin, likely to dispose and prepare us to be sincere Penitents when we grow old? Do we not see that a Custom of Sinning, in some Men, destroys the Modesty of human Nature; in others, all Sense of God and of Religion, or of the natural Differences of Good and Evil? Some Men sin on till they despise Repentance; others, till they think Repentance is too late; so that though Men were sure that they should live long enough to grow wiser, and to repent and reform the Sins and Extravagancies of Youth, yet no Man, who enters upon a wicked Course of Life, has any Reason to expect that he shall ever repent: And therefore it is extremely dangerous to flatter ourselves into a Habit and Custom of sinning, with the Hopes and Expectations that we shall live to repent of our Sins; and if this be dangerous, it must be very dangerous to flatter ourselves with the Hopes of long Life, which is the great Temptation to Men to sin on, and to delay their Repentance till old Age.

2. Since

2. Since the Time of our Death is so unknown and uncertain to us, we ought always to live in Expectation of it; to be so far from promising ourselves long Life, that we should not promise ourselves a Day: And the Reason of it is plain and necessary, because we are not sure of a Day.

This, you'll say, is hard indeed, to live always in Expectation of Dying, which is no better than dying every Day, or enduring the repeated Fears and Terrors of Death every Day, which is the most uncomfortable Part of Dying; at this rate we never live, but instead of Dying once, as God has appointed, we are always Dying; nay, this indeed is a fine Saying, but signifies nothing; for no Man does it, nor can do it; though we may die every Day, we see that Men live on forty, fifty, threescore Years; and therefore, though we know that our Lives are uncertain, yet no Man can think every Day, that he shall die to Day.

This is very true, and therefore to live always in Expectation of Dying, does not signify a Belief that we shall die To-day, but only that we may; which answers the Objection against the Uncomfortableness of it; for such an Expectation as this, has nothing of Dread and Terror in it, but only Prudence and Caution. Men may live very comfortably, and enjoy all the innocent Pleasures of Life with these Thoughts about them. To
expect

A Practical Discourse

expect Death every Day, is like expecting Thieves every Night; which does not disturb our Rest, but only makes us lock and bar our Doors, and provide for our own Defence. Thus to expect Death, is not to live under the perpetual Fears of dying, but to live as a wise Man would do, who knows, not that he *must*, but that he *may* die To-day.

That is to be always prepared for Death: Not to defer our Repentance and Return to God one Moment; not to commit any wilful Sin, lest Death should surprize us in it; not to be slothful and negligent, but to be always employed in our Master's Business, according to our Saviour's Counsel, *Luke* xii. 35, &c. *Let your loins be girded about, and your lights burning; and ye yourselves like unto men that wait for the Lord, when he will return from the wedding; that when he cometh and knocketh, they may open unto him immediately. Blessed are those servants, whom the Lord when he cometh shall find watching. And this know, that if the good man of the house had known what hour the thief would come, he would have watched, and not suffered his house to be broke through. Be ye therefore ready also, for the Son of Man cometh at an hour when ye think not.* This our Saviour also warns us of, in the Parable of the wise and foolish Virgins, *Math.* xxv. *While the Bridegroom tarried, they all slept; but the wise Virgins presently arose, and trimmed their Lamps;*

and

and went in with him to the Marriage, and the Door was shut; the foolish Virgins had no Oil, and their Lamps were gone out; and while they went to buy Oil, they were shut out, and could afterwards procure no Admission. *Watch therefore, for ye know neither the day nor the hour when the Son of Man cometh.*

This is the Danger of a sudden Death, and the Reason why our Church prays against it; for were we always in a Preparation to die, with our Lamps trimmed and burning, like Virgins who expect the Bridegroom, to die then without Notice, without Fear and Apprehension, without the melancholy Solemnities of dying, were a true εὐθανασία, the most desirable Way of dying: But the Danger of a sudden Death is, that Men are surprized in their Sins, and hurried away to Judgment, before their Accounts are ready; that they are snatched out of this World, before they have made any Provisions for the next; and the only Way to prevent this, is to be always upon our Watch, always in Expectation of Death, and always prepared for it.

Some Men think themselves very safe, if after an Age of Sin and Vanity, they have but so much Notice of Death, as to ask God's Pardon upon a sick Bed, to confess and bewail the Wickedness of their past Lives, to die in Horrors and Agonies of Mind, which they call Repentance; but indeed are nothing else but the sad Presages of an awakened Conscience,

science, distracted with its own Guilt, and the terrible Expectations of Vengeance. But tho' this be a very comfortless way of dying, and, I fear, generally very hopeless too; yet no Man can promise himself so much as this, who does not live in a constant Expectation of Death. We may be cut off by a sudden Stroke, or seized with Distraction or Stupidness, that if only asking God Pardon before we die would save our Souls, we could not do it: And this is the Case of so many Sinners, that it should be a Warning to all. Men who know not when, or how, or in what Manner they must die, ought to be ready prepared against all Accidents, and surprizing Events.

3. Since the Time of our Death is so very uncertain, it concerns us to improve our present Time; because no Time is ours but what is present. I observed before, that the Shortness of our Lives, though we were to live to the utmost Extent of them, threescore and ten, or fourscore Years, was a sufficient Reason to lose none of our Time, but to improve it to the best and wisest Purposes: And the surest Way to lose none of our Time, is to improve the present Time; and there is a plain necessary Reason why we should do that, because our Lives are uncertain; and therefore no Time is ours, but what is present. The Time past was ours; but that is gone, and we can never recal it, nor live it over again:

gain: If we have spent it well, we shall find it ours still in our Account, but it is no longer our Time to live and act in. The Time to come may be ours, and may not; because we know not whether we shall live to it, and therefore we cannot reckon upon it. The Time present is ours, and that is the only Time that is ours; and therefore if we will improve our Time, we must improve our present Time, we must live To-day, and not put off living 'till To-morrow.

All Mankind are sensible of the Necessity and Prudence of this in all other Matters, excepting the Concernments of their Souls. An *Epicurean* Sensualist is for the present Gratification of his Lusts; *Vive hodie*, is his Motto; *Let us eat and drink, for to-morrow we die*. Men who are intent upon increasing Riches, and advancing their Fortunes and Honours, are for taking the present Time and Opportunity to do it. Indeed, setting aside the Consideration of the Uncertainty of our Lives, there are some Things which a wise Man will not delay, or put off to another Time, when he has Opportunity to do it at present.

What is necessary to be done, he will do as soon as he can; the very first Moment that it becomes necessary, if Opportunity serves.

What is necessary every Day, he will not put off from one Day to another, but will do it every Day; as eating, and drinking, and sleeping are.

What

What he resolves to do, and may as well do at present, and is as fit to be done at present, as at any other Time, he will do at present.

What may suffer by Delays, he will do the first time he can do it.

What is proper for peculiar Times and Seasons, he will do when those Times and Seasons come; as the Husbandman observes the Seasons for sowing and reaping; the Tradesman his Markets and Fairs.

What is of present Use and Convenience to him, what he takes great Pleasure in, or what he mightily longs for and desires, he will by no means delay, but is doing at present.

Now all these are very weighty Reasons why we should take care of our Souls, repent of our Sins, live in the Practice of all Christian Graces and Virtues, and do all the Good we can at present; but much more, when we consider that our Lives are so uncertain, that we may have no other Time to do any thing of this in, but what is present.

For, 1. Is any thing of more absolute Necessity, than the Salvation of our Souls? This is that one Thing needful; the Salvation of our Souls is needful, as a necessary End; and the Practice of true Religion needful, as subservient to that End. If to escape eternal Misery, and to obtain eternal Happiness, be not necessary, I know not what can make any thing necessary. And if this cannot be done without the Knowledge and Practice of true Religion, that

is

is as necessary as the Salvation of our Souls is: And can any present Time, how early soever it be, be too soon to do that which is necessary to be done? Especially when we are not sure of any other Time to do it in: No Time is too soon to do that which is absolutely necessary; and no wise Man will neglect doing that at present, which unless it be done, he must be miserable for ever; and yet it may never be done, if it be not done at present.

2. Is not Religion, and the Care of our Souls, the Work of every Day, as much as eating and drinking to preserve our bodily Health and Strength is? Must we not pray to God every Day, and make his Laws the Rule of our Actions every Day, and repent of our Sins, and do what Good we can every Day? And what is the Work of every Day, we ought to do every Day, though we were secure of living till To-morrow; much more when we know that we may die before another Day comes.

3. Do ye not all resolve to repent of your Sins, and reform your Lives, before ye die? And is it not as necessary to repent of your Sins To-day, as ever it will be? Is not To-day as proper a Time to repent in, as ever you are likely to have? Are you sure of having another Day to repent in, if you neglect this? This may convince any considering Man, That no Resolutions, of repenting hereafter,

can be sincere; because such Men resolve indeed to repent, but do not resolve to do it at such a Time when they can do it; that is, the present Time, which alone they are sure of; but put it off till another Time, which may never be theirs.

I grant, Men may sincerely resolve to do that hereafter, a Month, or half a Year, or a Year hence, which they do not think so fitting and convenient to do at present: But then, this is not an absolute Resolution to do such a Thing, but a conditional Resolution, that they will do it, if they live till such a Time, when it will be convenient to be done.

Consider then which of these you mean, when you resolve to repent: Is it only a conditional Resolution, that you will repent, if you live till such a Time? I grant, there is some Sense in this Resolution; but I wish you would consider what Danger there is in it too. For are you contented to be eternally miserable, if you do not live till your Time of Repentance comes? No, this you tremble at the Thoughts of; and resolve to repent, because you resolve not to be miserable for ever. That is, you absolutely resolve to repent; you are convinced this is absolutely necessary; it is a Work that must be done, and you are resolved to do it. Consider then, how vain and contradictory this Resolution is, to resolve *to repent hereafter*.

Which

Which is an absolute Resolution, with a Condition annexed to it, and a very uncertain one too: A Resolution certainly to repent, but not in a certain but uncertain Time. And yet those who repent, must repent in some Time; and Repentance can never be certain, when the Time to repent is uncertain. Indeed no Resolution is good, which is not for the present Time, when there are no Exceptions against doing it at present, especially when there is such manifest Danger in deferring it. To resolve to repent hereafter, when the present Time is the only certain Time to repent in, only signifies that Men are convinced of the Necessity of Repentance, but love their Sins so well, that they cannot part with them yet; and therefore that they may sin on securely, without the perpetual Fears and Terrors of another World, they resolve to repent hereafter. Now though there were no such manifest Danger in a Delay, from the Uncertainty of our Lives; yet let any Man judge, whether such Resolutions as these are like ever to take Effect: A Resolution which is owing to a great Love to Sin, and is intended only to silence Mens guilty Fears, and give them a present Security in sinning. For this Reason they resolve not to repent now, but to repent hereafter; and if they keep this Resolution, they will never repent: For their *hereafter* will never come; which does not signify any set and determined

A Practical DISCOURSE

sincere; because such Men resolve
repent, but do not resolve to do
Time when they can do it; tha
esent Time, which alone they are
ut put it off till another Time,
never be theirs.
grant, Men may sincerely resolve
hereafter, a Month, or half a Y
ear hence, which they do not thin
g and convenient to do at prese
en, this is not an absolute Resoluti
ich a Thing, but a conditional R
hat they will do it, if they live
a Time, when it will be conveni
done.

Consider then which of the
when you resolve to repent:
ditional Resolution, that y
you live till such a Tim
some Sense in this P
you would consider
it too. For
ly miserable,
Time of R
tremble ?
repent.
rable
so
ab
be done,
sider then,
Resolution is, to

termined Time, but any Time which is not present. The Reason why they resolve not to repent To-day, will extend to every Day when it comes; that is, that they love their Sins, and are unwilling to part with them: And the Reason why they resolve to repent hereafter, will serve for all hereafters, but will never serve for any Time present; *viz.* because they will not repent yet, and yet will flatter themselves into Security with the vain Hopes of Repentance. Flatter not yourselves then with vain Hopes; he who resolves to repent, but does not resolve to repent presently, though he knows he is sure of no other Time but the present to repent in, does not sincerely resolve to repent, but only resolves to delay his Repentance.

The like may be said concerning the Danger of Delays, concerning missing the proper Times and Seasons of Action, and neglecting that which is of present Use to us, and which we ought above all Things to desire, *viz.* to secure the Happiness of our immortal Souls; but I shall only add this one Thing to make you sensible what it is to let slip the present Time, without improving it to any wise Purposes: That he who loses his present Time, loses all the Time he has, all the Time that he can call his own; which is the Sum of all other Arguments. That the present Time is the only Time he has to live in, to repent in, to serve God, and to do

good

good to Men in, to improve his Knowledge, and to exercise his Graces, and to prepare himself for a blessed Immortality; which are the most necessary, the most useful, the most desirable Things in the World; and that which gives the Value to Time itself, which is valuable only for the Sake of what may be done, and what may be enjoyed in it.

But you'll say, At this rate, we must spend our whole Lives in the Duties of Religion, in thinking of God and another World, in Acts of Repentance and Mortification, in Prayer and Fasting, and such like Exercises of Devotion; here will be no Time left for the ordinary Affairs of Life, scarce to eat or drink, or sleep in; but that they will have some of our Time, whether we will or no: But here is no Allowance made for Recreations and Diversions, for the Conversation of Friends, and innocent Mirth and Pastime, to refresh our wearied Bodies and Minds. For if we must be so careful to improve the present Time to the best Purposes, our present Time is our whole Time; for we have no Time but what is present; and as one Minute succeeds another, still we must improve it to the best Purposes; that is, we can do but one Thing all our Lives, and the best Way then would be to turn Hermits, and sequester ourselves from the World and Human Conversation.

The Answer to this Objection, will teach us what it is to improve our present Time, and how it must be done.

Now, 1. I allow the Objection so far, that if a Man have mis-spent great Part of his Life, have contracted great Guilt, and powerful Habits of Vice; the chief, and almost the only Thing such a Man can do, is to bewail his Sins before God, and with earnest and repeated Importunities to beg his pardon: To live in a State of Penance and Mortification; to deny himself the Pleasures and Comforts of Life, 'till he has in some measure subdued his Love of Sin, and regained the Command and Government of his Passions, and has recovered the Peace of his Mind, and some good Hopes that God has forgiven him, and received him into Favour for the Sake of Christ. Thus he ought to do; and when he is made thoroughly sensible of his Sins, and the Danger he is in, he can do no otherwise. While he is terrified with the Fears of Hell, he has little Stomach to the necessary Affairs and Business of Life, much less to the Mirth and Pleasures of it. But this is such an Interruption to the ordinary and regular Course of Life, as a Fit of Sickness is, which confines us to our Bed, or to our Chamber, and makes us incapable of minding any thing but the Recovery of our Health: And when this is the Case, then indeed the Care of our Souls is the only necessary Business, and the only Employment of our Time.

2. But when this is not the Case, the wise Improvement of our present Time does not confine us always to be on our Knees; or doing something which has a direct and immediate Aspect upon God and another World; for the State of this World will not admit of that: But he employs his Time well, who divides it among all the Affairs and Offices of Life, between this World and the next; and employs the several Portions of his Time in Things fit and proper for such a Season; who begins and ends the Day with adoring his Maker and Redeemer, blessing him for all his Mercies both temporal and spiritual; begging the Pardon of all his Sins, the Protection of his Providence, the Assistance of his Grace; and then minds his secular Affairs with Justice and Righteousness, eats and drinks with Sobriety and Temperance, does all good Offices for Men as Occasion serves; and if he have any spare Time, improves it for the Increase of his Knowledge, by reading and meditating on the Scriptures, or other useful Books, or refreshes himself with the innocent and chearful Conversation of his Friends, or such other Diversions as are not so much a Loss and Expence of Time, as a necessary Relaxation of the Mind to recruit our Spirits, and to make us more fit either for Business or Devotion. But then on Days

set apart for the more publick and solemn Acts of Worship, Religion is his chief Employment; for that is the proper Work of the Day, to worship God, and to examine the State of his own Soul; to learn his Duty more perfectly; and to affect his Mind with such a powerful Sense of God, and another World, as may arm him against all Temptations, when he returns to this World again. This is to improve our present Time well, to observe the proper Times and Seasons of Action, and to do what is fit and proper for such Seasons; never to do any Thing which is evil; and as for the several Kinds of good Actions, to do what particular Times and Seasons require. Thus we may give a good Account of our whole Time, even of our most loose and vacant Hours; which it becomes us to do, tho' we were certain to live many Years, but does more nearly concern us when our Time is so uncertain.

4. Since our Lives are so very uncertain, this ought to cure an anxious Care and Solicitude for Times to come. We may live many Years, though our Lives are uncertain, and therefore a provident Care becomes us; but we may die also very quickly, and why then should we disturb ourselves with Tomorrow's Care, much less with some remoter Possibilities? Hast thou at any Time an ill Prospect before thee of private or publick Calamities? Do the Storms gather? Are the Clouds

Clouds black and lowring, and charged with Thunder, and ready to break over thy Head? Shelter thyself as well as thou canst; make all prudent Provision for a Storm, because thou may'st live to see it: But be not too much dismayed and terrified with a Storm at a Distance; for thy Head may be lain low enough, and out of its Reach, before it breaks; and then all this Trouble and Perplexity is in vain. Many such Examples have I seen, of Men disturbed with ill Presages of what was coming, which besides that those Things did not happen which they expected, or were not so black and dismal as their affrighted Fancy painted them; if they had come, they were very safe first, and got out of their Way.

I do not intend by this to comfort Men against foreseen Evils, that they may die before they come; which is a small Comfort to most Men, when it may be, Death is the most formidable Thing in the Evils they fear; but since our Lives are uncertain, and we may die and never see the Evils we fear; it is unreasonable to be as much distracted with them, as if they were present and certain. The Uncertainty of future Events, is one Reason why we ought not to be anxious and follicitous about them; and the Uncertainty of our Lives is another: And what is so very uncertain, ought not to be the Object of any great Concern or Passion.

5. For

5. For the same Reason we ought not to be greatly afraid of Men, nor to put our Trust and Confidence in them, because their Lives are very uncertain: They may not be able to hurt us when we are most apprehensive of Danger from them; nor to help us, when we need them most: This is the Psalmist's Argument, *Psal.* cxlvi. 3, 4. *Put not your trust in princes, nor in the son of man, in whom there is no help: His breath goeth forth, he returneth to his earth: In that very day his thoughts perish.* Isa. ii. 22. *Cease ye from man, whose breath is in his nostrils, for wherein is he to be accounted of?* Men, especially great and powerful Men, may do us a great deal of Hurt, and may do us a great deal of Good; and therefore common Prudence will teach us, by all wise and honest Arts, to gain their Favour, and to avoid all unreasonable and needless Provocations: But yet at best they are such brittle Creatures, that they can be the Objects only of a subordinate Fear or Hope. When the Fear of Man comes in Competition with the Fear of God, it is a wise Counsel which the Prophet *Isaiah* gives, *Say ye not, A confederacy, to all them to whom this people shall say, A confederacy; neither fear ye their fear, nor be afraid. Sanctify the Lord God of Hosts himself, and let him be your fear, and let him be your dread; and he shall be for a sanctuary,* Isa. viii. 12, 13, 14. There is a vast Difference between the Power of God and Men;

which

which is our Saviour's Reason why we should fear God more than Man: *Be not afraid of them that kill the body, and after that have no more that they can do; but I will forewarn ye whom ye shall fear: Fear him, which after he hath killed, hath power to cast into Hell; yea, I say unto you, fear him,* Luke xii. 4, 5. But whatever Power Men may have to hurt while they live, they can do us no Hurt when they are dead; and their Lives are so very uncertain, that we may be quickly eased of those Fears. The same may be said with respect to Hope and Confidence in Men; tho' their Word and Promise were always sacred, yet their Lives are uncertain; *Their breath goeth forth, they return to the earth; in that very day their thoughts perish;* all the Good, and all the Evil they intend to do: But *happy is he that hath the God of Jacob for his help, whose hope is in the Lord his God, which made heaven and earth, the sea and all that therein is, who keepeth truth for ever,* Psalm. cxlvi. 5, 6.

6. For a Conclusion of this Argument, I shall briefly vindicate the Wisdom and Goodness of God, in concealing from us the Time of our Death. This we are very apt to complain of, that our Lives are so very uncertain, that we know not To-day, but that we may die To-morrow; and we would be mighty glad to meet with any one who would certainly inform us in this Matter, how long we are

to

to live: But if we think a little better of it, we shall be of another Mind.

For, 1. Though I presume many of you would be glad to know that you shall certainly live twenty, or thirty, or forty Years longer; yet would it be any Comfort to know, that you must die To-morrow, or some few Months, or a Year or two hence? which may be your Case for ought you know; and this I believe you are not very desirous to know; for how would this chill your Blood and Spirits? How would it overcast all the Pleasures and Comforts of Life? You would spend your Days like Men under the Sentence of Death, while the Execution is suspended.

Did all Men, who must die young, certainly know it, it would destroy the Industry and Improvements of half Mankind, which would half destroy the World, or be an insupportable Mischief to human Societies: For what Man, who knows that he must die at twenty, or five and twenty, a little sooner or later, would trouble himself with ingenious or gainful Arts, or concern himself any more with this World, than just to live so long in it? And yet how necessary is the Service of such Men in the World? What great Things do they many times do? And what great Improvements do they make? How pleasant and diverting is their Conversation, while it is innocent? How do they enjoy

enjoy themselves, and give Life and Spirit to the graver Age? How thin would our Schools, our Shops, our Univerſities, and all Places of Education be, did they know how little Time many of them were to live in the World? For would ſuch Men concern themſelves to learn the Arts of Living, who muſt die as ſoon as they have learnt them? Would any Father be at a great Expence in educating his Child, only that he might die with a little *Latin* and *Greek*, Logick and Philoſophy? No, half the World muſt be divided into Cloiſters and Nunneries, and Nurſeries for the Grave.

Well, you'll ſay, ſuppoſe that, and is not this an Advantage above all the Inconveniencies you can think of, to ſecure the Salvation of ſo many Thouſands who are now eternally ruined by youthful Luſts and Vanities, but would ſpend their Days in Piety and Devotion, and make the next World their only Care, if they knew how little while they were to live here?

Right: I grant this might be a good Way to correct the Heat and Extravagancies of Youth, and ſo it would be to ſhew them Heaven and Hell; but God does not think fit to do either, becauſe it offers too much Force and Violence to Mens Minds; it is no Trial of their Virtue, of their Reverence for God, of their Conqueſts and Victory over this World by the Power of Faith, but makes

This would take off all Restraints from Men, and give free Scope to their vicious Inclinations, when they knew, that how wicked soever they were, they should not die before their Time was come, and could never be surprized by Death, since they certainly knew when it will come, which destroys one great Motive to Obedience, that Sin shall shorten Mens Lives, and that Virtue and Piety should prolong them: That *the wicked shall not live out half their days:* That *the fear of the Lord prolongeth days; but the years of the wicked shall be shortened,* Prov. x. 27. Such Promises and Threatnings as these must be struck out of the Bible, should God let all Men know the Time of their Death.

Nay, this would frustrate the Methods and Designs of Providence for the reclaiming Sinners. Sometimes publick Calamities, Plague, and Famine, and Sword, alarm a wicked World, and summon Men to Repentance; sometimes a dangerous Fit of Sickness awakens Men into a Sense of their Sins, and works in them a true and lasting Repentance; but all this would be ineffectual, did Men know the Time of their Death, and that such publick Judgments, or threatning Sickness, should not kill them.

The Uncertainty of our Lives is a great Motive to constant Watchfulness, to an early and persevering Piety; but to know when we shall die, could serve no good End, but would

increase

increase the Wickedness of Mankind, which is too great already; which is a sufficient Vindication of the Wisdom of God in leaving the Time of Death unknown and uncertain to us.

SECT. VI.

That we must die but once; or that Death translates us to an unchangeable State: With the Improvement of it.

THE last Thing to be considered is, That we must die but once: *It is appointed for men* once *to die*. There are some Exceptions from this Rule, as there are from Dying; That as *Enoch* and *Elias* did not die, so some have been raised again from the Dead, to live in this World; and such Men died twice. But this is a certain Rule in general, That as all Men must die *once*, so they must die *but once*; which needs no other Proof, but the daily Experience and Observation of Mankind.

But that which I intend by it is this; That once Dying determines our State and Condition for ever: When we put off these mortal Bodies, we must not return into them again to act over a new Part in this World, and to correct the Errors and Miscarriages of our former Lives: Death translates us to an immutable and unchangeable State; that in this

O Sense

Senfe what the Wife Man tells us is true: *If the tree fall towards the fouth, or towards the north, in the place where the tree falleth, there it fhall be.* Ecclef. xi. 3. This is a Confideration of very great Moment, and deferves to be more particularly explained, which I fhall do in the following Propofitions.

1. That this Life is the only State of Trial and Probation for Eternity: And therefore,
2. Death, whenever it comes, as it puts a final Period to this Life, that we die once for all, and muft never live again, as we do now in this World; fo it puts a final End to our Work too, that our Day of Grace, and Time of working for another World, ends with this Life. And, 3. As a neceffary Confequence of both thefe, once Dying puts us into an immutable and unchangeable State.

1. That this Life only is our State of Trial and Probation for Eternity; whatever is to be done by us, to obtain the Favour of God, and a bleffed Immortality, muft be done in this Life.

I obferved before, that this Life is wholly in order to the next; that the great, the only neceffary Bufinefs, we have to do in this World, is to fit and prepare ourfelves to live for ever in GOD's Prefence; *To finifh the work GOD has given us to do,* that we may receive the Reward of Good and Faithful Servants, to enter into our Mafter's Reft: I now add, That the only Time we have to do this in, is

while

while we live in this World. This is evident from what St. *Paul* tells us, That *we muſt all appear before the judgment-ſeat of Chriſt, that every one may receive the things done in his body, according to what he hath done, whether it be good or bad.* 2 Cor. v. 10. Now if we muſt be judged, and receive our final Sentence according to what we have done in the Body, then our only Time of Trial and Working, is while we live in theſe Bodies; for the future Judgment relates only to what is done in the Body.

The Goſpel of Chriſt is the Rule whereby we muſt be judged, even that Goſpel which St. *Paul* preached, *Rom.* ii. 16. And all the Laws and Precepts of the Goſpel, concern the Government of our Converſation in this World; and therefore if we be judged by the Goſpel, we muſt be judged only for what we have done in this World.

This Life, throughout the Scripture, is repreſented as the Time of Working; as a Race, a Warfare, a labouring in the Vineyard; the other World, as a Place of Recompence, of Rewards or Puniſhments. And if there be ſuch a Relation between this World and the next, as between fighting and conquering and receiving the Crown, as between running a Race, and obtaining a Prize, as between the Work and the Reward; then we muſt fight and conquer, run our Race, and finiſh our

Work in this World, if we expect the Rewards of the next.

Many of those Graces and Virtues, which our Saviour has promised to reward with eternal Life, can be exercised only in this World: Faith and Hope are peculiar only to this Life, while the other World is absent and unseen. And these are the great Principles and Graces of the Christian Life, to believe what we do not see, and to live and act upon the Hopes of future Rewards: The Government of our bodily Appetites and Passions, by the Rules of Temperance, Sobriety, and Chastity, necessarily supposes that we have Bodies, and bodily Appetites and Passions to govern; and therefore these Virtues can be exercised only while we live in these Bodies, which follicit and tempt us to sensual Excesses. To live above this World, to despise the tempting Glories of it, is a Virtue only while we live in it, and are tempted by it: To have our Conversation in Heaven, which is the most divine Temper of Mind, is a Gospel-Grace only while we live in this World, at a great Distance from Heaven: To be contented in all Conditions, to trust God in the greatest Dangers, to suffer patiently for Righteousness Sake, &c. I need not tell you, are Virtues proper only for this World; for there can be no Exercise for them in Heaven, unless we can think it a Virtue to be patient and contented

tented with the Happiness and Glory of that blessed Place.

Thus most of the Sins which the Gospel forbids under the Penalty of eternal Damnation, can be committed by us only in this World, and in these Bodies; such as Fornication, Adultery, Uncleanness, Rioting, Drunkenness, Injustice, Murder, Theft, Oppression of the Poor and Fatherless, earthly Pride and Ambition, Covetousness, a fond Idolatry of this World, Disobedience to Parents and Governors, &c. Now if these be the Things for which Men shall be saved or damned, it is certain that Men must be saved or damned only for what they do in this Life.

Bad Men, who are fond of this World, and of bodily Pleasures, which makes them impatient of the severe Restraints of Religion, complain very much of this; that their eternal Happiness or Misery depends upon such a short and uncertain Life: That they must spend this Life under the Awe and Terror of the next: That some few momentary Pleasures must be punished with endless Misery; and that if they outslip their Time of Repentance, if they venture to sin on too long, or die a little too soon, there is no Remedy for them for ever.

But let bad Men look to this, and consider the Folly of their Choice: I am sure, how hard soever it may be thought to be eternally damned for the short Pleasures of Sin, no Man can reasonably think it a hard Condition of eternal Salvation, to spend a short Life in the Service of God. And if we will allow, that God may justly require our Services and Obedience for so great a Reward as Heaven is; where can we do him this Service but on Earth? If a corrupt Nature must be cleansed and purified; if an earthly Nature must be spiritualized and refined, before it can be fit to live in Heaven: Where can this be done but on Earth, while we live in these Bodies of Flesh, and are encompassed with sensible Objects? This is the Time for a divine Soul, which aspires after Immortality, to raise itself above the Body, to conquer this present World, by the Belief and Hope of unseen Things; to awaken and exercise its spiritual Powers and Faculties, and to adorn itself with those Graces and Virtues which come down from Heaven, and by the Mercies of God, and the Merits of our Saviour, will carry us up thither. There is no middle State, between living in this Body, and out of it; and therefore whatever Habits and Dispositions of Mind are necessary to make a Spirit happy when it goes out of this Body, must be formed and exercised while it is in it. Earth and Heaven are two Extremes, and opposite States of Life, and therefore it is impossible immediately to pass from one to t'other: A Soul which is wholly sensualized by living in the Body, if it be turned out of the Body without

out any Change, cannot afcend into Heaven, which is a State of perfect Purity; for in all Reafon, the Place and State of Life muft be fitted to the Nature of Things: And therefore a Life of Holinefs, while we live in thefe Bodies, is a kind of middle State between Earth and Heaven; fuch a Man belongs to both Worlds, he is united to this World by his Body, which is made of Earth, and feels the Impreffion of fenfible Objects, but his Heart and Affections are in Heaven: By Faith he contemplates thofe invifible Glories, and feels and relifhes the Pleafures of a heavenly Life. And he who has his Converfation in Heaven while he lives in this Body, is ready prepared and fitted to afcend thither, when he goes out of it; he paffeth from Earth to Heaven through the middle Region (if I may fo fpeak) of a holy and divine Life.

Befides this, it was neceffary to the Happinefs and good Government of this prefent World, that future Rewards or Punifhments fhould have Relation to the Good or Evil which we do in this Life. This in many Cafes lays Reftraints upon the Lufts and Paffions of Men, when the Rods and Axes of Princes cannot reach them; it over-awes them with invifible Terrors, and makes a guilty Confcience its own Judge and Tormentor: It fowres all the Pleafures of Sin, ftuffs the Adulterer's Pillow with Thorns, and mingles Gall and Wormwood with the Drunkard's Cups:

Cups: It governs thofe who are under no other Government; whofe boundlefs and uncontroulable Power gives them Opportunity of doing what Mifchief they pleafe, and gives them Impunity in doing it. But the moft lawlefs Tyrants, who fear no other Power, yet feel the invifible Reftraints of Confcience, and thofe fecret and fevere Rebukes which make them tremble. Nay, many times the Fear of the other World governs thofe, whom no prefent Evil or Punifhment could govern: Men who would venture whatever they could fuffer in this Life by their Sins, are yet afraid of Hell, and dare not venture that: Thofe who would venture being fick after a Debauch; who would venture to facrifice their Bodies, their Eftates, their Reputation, in the Service of their Lufts; who are contented to take their Fortune at the Gallows, or at the Whipping-poft; yet dare not venture Lakes of Fire and Brimftone, the Worm that never dieth, and the Fire that never goeth out.

Thus on the other hand, How much is it for the prefent Happinefs of the World, that Men fhould live in the Practice of thofe Chriftian Graces and Virtues, which no human Laws command, and the Neglect of which no human Laws will punifh? As to inftance only in the Love of Enemies, and Forgivenefs of Injuries, and fuch an univerfal Charity, as does all the Good it can to all Men: I need

need not prove that the Exercise of these Virtues is for the Good of the World; or that no human Laws require the Exercise of them, in such noble Measures and Degrees, as the Gospel does.

The Laws of the Land allow Scope enough to satisfy the most revengeful Man who will use all the Extremities and all the vexatious Arts of Prosecution, unless nothing will satisfy his Revenge, but Blood and a speedy Execution: For the Laws ought to punish those Injuries which a good Christian ought to forgive; and then some Men may be undone by legal Revenge, and others damned for taking it. If no Man should do any good Offices for others, but what the Law commands, there would be very little Good done in the World; for Laws are principally intended for the Preservation of Justice; but the Acts of a generous and bountiful Charity are free: And Men may be as charitable as the Law requires, without any Degree of that divine Charity, which will carry them to Heaven. Nothing but the Hopes and Fears of the next World can enforce these Duties on us: And this justifies the Wisdom and Goodness of God, in making the present Exercise of these Virtues necessary to our future Rewards. I shall only add, That whatever Complaints bad Men may make, that their future Happiness or Misery depends upon the Government and Conduct of their Lives in this World, I am sure all Mankind

immortal Life, which is begun in this World, and will be perfected in the next; which is the Sum of St. *Paul*'s Argument, *ver.* 6, 7, 8, 9, 10, 11. Thus he tells us, *Rom.* viii. 10, 11. *If Christ be in you, the body is dead because of sin; but the spirit is life, because of righteousness:* That is, our Bodies are mortal, and must die, by an irreversible Sentence which God pronounced against *Adam* when he had sinned; but the Soul and Spirit has a new Principle of Life, a Principle of Righteousness and Holiness; by which it lives to God, and therefore cannot fall into a State of Death when the Body dies; *But if the Spirit of him that raised up Jesus from the dead, dwell in you; he that raised up Christ from the dead shall also quicken your mortal bodies, by his Spirit that dwelleth in you.* That is, when the divine Spirit has quickened our Souls, and raised them into a new Life, though our Bodies must die, yet the same divine Spirit will raise them up also into immortal Life.

This is the plain Account of the Matter: If Death arrests us while we are in a State of Sin and Death, we must die for ever: But if our Souls are alive to God by a Principle of Grace and Holiness, before our Bodies die, they must live for ever. A dead Soul must die with its Body; that is, sink into a State of Misery, which is the Death, and the Loss of the Soul: A living Soul survives the Body in a State of Bliss and Happiness, and
shall

shall receive its Body again, glorious and immortal, at the Resurrection of the Just. But this Change of State must be made while we live in these Bodies. A dead Soul cannot revive in the other World, nor a living Soul die there; and therefore this Life is the Day of God's Grace and Patience, the next World is the Place of Judgment. And the Reason St. *Peter* gives why God is not hasty in executing Judgment, *but is long suffering to us-ward*, is, because he is *not willing that any should perish, but that all should come to repentance.* 2 Pet. iii. 5. Hence the Apostle to the *Hebrews* exhorts them, *Wherefore as the Holy Ghost saith, To-day if ye will hear his voice, harden not your hearts, as in the provocation, in the day of temptation in the wilderness, when your fathers tempted me, proved me, and saw my works forty years. Wherefore I was grieved with that generation, and said, They do always err in their hearts; and they have not known my ways. So I sware in my wrath, they shall not enter into my rest.* Heb. iii. 7, 8, 9, 10, 11.

There is some Dispute, what is meant by *To-day,* whether it be the Day of this Life, or such a fixed and determined Day and Season of Grace, as may end long before this Life: The Example of the *Israelites,* of whom God did swear in his Wrath, that they should die in the Wilderness, and never enter into his Rest, that is, into the Land of *Canaan,*

seems

seems to incline it to the latter Sense; for this Sentence, *that they should not enter into his rest*, was pronounced against them long before they died; for which Reason they wandered forty Years in the Wilderness, till all that Generation of Men were dead; and if we are concerned in this Example, then we also may provoke God to such a Degree, that he may pronounce the final Sentence on us, That we should never enter into Heaven, long before we leave this World. Our Day of Grace may have a shorter Period than our Lives, and we may wander about in this World as the *Israelites* did in the Wilderness, under an irreversible Doom and Sentence. And the Scope of the Apostle's Argument seems to require this Sense, which is to engage them to a speedy Repentance, *To-day if ye will hear his voice, harden not your hearts:* But why *To-day?* Is it because our Lives are uncertain, and we may die before To-morrow? No, but *lest we provoke God to swear in his wrath, that we shall not enter into his rest*.

All Men know, that if they die in a State of Sin, they must be miserable for ever; and this is a Reason to repent before they die: But the Apostle seems to argue farther, That by their Delays and repeated Provocations, they may tempt God to shorten their Day of Grace, and pronounce an irrevocable Sentence on them, which leaves no place for Repentance; which elsewhere he enforces from
the

the Example of *Esau*, who sold his Birthright, Heb. xii. 15, 16, 17. *Looking diligently, lest any man fail of the grace of God; lest any root of bitterness springing up, trouble you, and thereby many be defiled; lest there be any fornicator, or prophane person, as Esau, who for one morsel of meat sold his birth-right. For ye know how that afterward when he would have inherited the blessing, he was rejected; for he found no place for repentance, though he sought it carefully with tears.*

The stating of this Matter may be thought a Digression from my present Design, but indeed it is not; for if by *To-day*, be meant the whole Time of this Life, that proves that Death puts a final Period to our Day of Grace; and if any shorter Period than this Life be meant by it, it proves it much stronger; for if our Sentence be passed before we die, it will not be revoked after Death. But the stating this Question is a Matter of so great Consequence to us, that if it were a Digression it were very pardonable; for many devout Minds, when they are disturbed and clouded with Melancholy, are afflicted with such Thoughts as these, That their Day of Grace is past, that God has sworn in his Wrath that they shall not enter into his Rest; and therefore their Repentance and Tears will be as fruitless as *Esau*'s were, which could not obtain the Blessing.

Now

Now for the resolving this Question, I shall say these three Things: 1. That the Day of Grace, according to the Terms of the Gospel, is commensurate with our Lives. 2. That notwithstanding this, Men may shorten their own Day of Grace, and God may in Wrath and Justice confirm the Sentence. 3. That the Reasons for lengthening the Day of Grace, together with our Lives, do not extend to the other World, and therefore Death must put a final Period to it.

1. That the Day of Grace, according to the Terms of the Gospel, is commensurate with our Lives; and there needs no other Proof of this, but that the Promise of Pardon and Forgiveness is made to all true Penitents, without any Limitation of Time: Whoever believes in Christ, and repents of his Sins, he shall be saved: This is the Doctrine of the Gospel; and if this be true, then it is certain, that at what time soever a Sinner sincerely repenteth of his Sins, he shall be saved; for otherwise some true and sincere Penitents, if they repent too late, after the Day of Grace is expired, shall be damned; and then it is not true, that all sincere Penitents shall be saved.

I know but one Objection against this, from the Example of *Esau*, who having sold his Birth-right, *when afterwards he would have inherited the blessing, was rejected; for he found no place for repentance, though he sought it it carefully with tears.* It seems then, that *Esau* repented too late, and so may we; his Repentance would not be accepted: And if we are concerned in this Example, as the Apostle intimates we are, then we may repent of our Sins when it is too late, and lose the Blessing as *Esau* did.

But this Objection is founded on a Mistake of *Esau*'s Case: The Repentance here mentioned is not *Esau*'s Repentance, but *Isaac*'s; that is, when *Isaac* had blessed *Jacob*, *Esau* with all his Tears and Importunity could not make him recal it: *i. e. Isaac* would not repent of the Blessing he had given to *Jacob*; *I have blessed him, yea, and he shall be blessed,* Gen. xxvii. 33.

Esau's Case then was not, that his Repentance came too late to be accepted, but that he could not obtain the Blessing, after he had sold his Birth-right, to which the Blessing was annexed. Now to apply this to the State of Christians; that which answers to *Esau*'s Birth-right, is their Right and Title to future Glory, being made the Sons of God by baptismal Regeneration, and Faith in Christ; to sell this Birth-right is to part with our Hopes of Heaven, for the Pleasures, or Riches, or Honours of this World, as *Esau* sold his Birth-right for one Morsel of Meat; that is, as the Apostle speaks, *to fail of the grace of God,* either through Unbelief, which he calls the *root of bitterness,* a renouncing the

Faith of Chrift, and returning to *Judaifm* or *Pagan* Idolatries, or by an impure and wicked Life: *Left there be any fornicator, or prophane perfon, as Efau, who for one morfel of meat fold his birth-right*; i. e. who defpifes the Hopes of Heaven for the finful Pleafures and tranfient Enjoyments of this World: Men who thus *fail of the grace of God*, and finally do fo, as *Efau* finally fold his Birthright, when our heavenly Father comes to give his Blefling, thofe great Rewards he has promifed in his Gofpel, how importunate foever they fhall then be for a Blefling, as *Efau* was, who *fought it carefully with tears*, they fhall *find no place for repentance*; God will not alter his Purpofes and Decrees for their Sakes. Our Saviour has given us a plain Comment on this, *Matth.* vii. 21, 22, 23. *Not every one that faith unto me, Lord, Lord, fhall enter into the kingdom of heaven; but he that doeth the will of my Father which is in heaven. Many will fay unto me at that day*; that is, the Day of Judgment, when the Blefling is to be given, *Lord, Lord, have we not prophefied in thy name, and in thy name caft out devils, and in thy name done many wonderful works?* Here is *Efau*'s Importunity for the Blefling. *And then will I profefs unto them, I never knew you: Depart from me, ye that work iniquity.* They were prophane *Efau's* who had fold their Birth-right for a Morfel of Meat, and now they found no place for Repentance:

pentance: Our Lord will not be perfuaded by all their Importunities to alter his Sentence, *but depart from me, ye that work iniquity.*

This Example then of *Esau* does not concern our prefent Cafe; it does not prove that a wicked Man, who hath fpent the greateft Part of his Life in Sin and Folly, fhall not be accepted and rewarded by God, if he fincerely repent of his Sins and reform his Life; but it only proves that a wicked and ungodly Chriftian, who prefers the Pleafures and Enjoyments of this World before the Hopes of Heaven, and defiles his Soul with impure and worldly Lufts, what Pretences foever he may make to the Bleffing, or how importunate foever he may be for it, fhall receive no Bleffing from God; that is, that *without holinefs no man fhall fee God*; which is the very Thing the Apoftle intended to prove by this Example, as you may fee, *ver.* 14.

I grant, the Cafe is different as to Churches and Nations; fometimes their Day of Grace is fixed and determined, beyond which, without Repentance, they fhall no longer enjoy the Light of the Gofpel. Thus the Appearance of Chrift in the Flefh, and his preaching the Gofpel to them, was the laft Trial of *Jerufalem*, and determined the Fate of that beloved City; and therefore when Chrift rode into *Jerufalem*, in order to his Crucifixion, *When he was come near, he beheld the city and wept*

wept over it, saying, if thou hadst known even thou, at least in this thy day, the things which belong unto thy peace! But now they are hid from thine eyes. For the days shall come upon thee, that thine enemies shall cast a trench about thee, and compass thee round, and keep thee in on every side, and shall lay thee even with the ground, and thy children within thee; and they shall not leave in thee one stone upon another: Because thou knewest not the time of thy visitation, Luke xix. 41, &c. And this our Saviour warned them of before, *John* xii. 35, 36. *Yet a little while is the light with you; walk while ye have the light, lest darkness come upon you: For he that walketh in darkness, knoweth not whither he goeth. While ye have light, believe in the light, that ye may be the children of light:* Which signifies, that unless they believed on him, while he was with them, they must be utterly destroyed: *The kingdom of God should be taken from them, and given to a nation bringing forth the fruits thereof;* as he proves by the Parable of the Housholder, who planted a Vineyard, *Matth.* xxi. 33, &c.

And this was in some measure the Case of the seven Churches of *Asia,* to whom St. *John* directed his Epistle, to summon them to Repentance, and to threaten them with the Removal of the Candlestick, if they did not repent. The Judgments of God in the Overthrow of some flourishing Churches, and in transplanting the Gospel from one Nation to another,

another, are very mysterious and unsearchable; but as for particular persons, who enjoy the Light of the Gospel, unless they shorten their Day of Grace themselves, God does not shorten it: As long as they live in this World, they are capable of Grace and Mercy if they truly repent.

2. Men may shorten their own Day of Grace; not by shortening the Time of Grace and Mercy, for that lasts as long as this Life does; but by out-living the Possibility of Repentance; and when they are past Repentance, their Day of Grace is at an end, and this may be much shorter than their Lives: That is, Men may so harden themselves in Sin, as to make their Repentance morally impossible; and God in his just and righteous Judgments may give up such Men to a State of Hardness and Impenitence.

Every Degree of Love to Sin, proportionably enslaves Men to the Practice of it; makes Repentance as uneasy and difficult, as it is *to pluck out a right eye, and cut off a right hand,* Matth. v. 29, 30. as painful as dying, as *crucifying the flesh with its affections and lusts,* which few Men will submit to, *Rom.* viii. 13. *Col.* iii. 5.

An Habit and Custom of Sin turns into Nature, and is as difficultly altered as Nature is: *Can the Ethiopian change his skin, or the leopard his spots? Then may you also do good, who are accustomed to do evil,* Jer. xiii. 23.

Some

Some Sins are of such a hardening Nature, that few Men who are once entangled by them, can ever break the Snare: Such as Adultery, the Love of strange Women, of whom *Solomon* tells us, *Her house inclineth unto death, and her paths unto the dead: None that go unto her return again, neither take they hold of the paths of life:* Prov. ii. 18, 19.

_{See Prov. v. 22, 23. vii. 22, 23. 26, 27.}

Covetousness is such another hardening Sin, that our Saviour tells us, *It is easier for a camel to go through the eye of a needle, than for a rich man to enter into heaven:* Those who love, and those who trust in their Riches, *Matth.* xiii. 23, 24, 25.

Those who have been once enlighten'd, and fall back again into Infidelity; who have been instructed in the Reasons of Faith, and the Motives of Obedience; who have had the heavenly Seed of God's Word sown in their Hearts, but have not brought forth the Fruits of it, are near the Curse of barren Ground, which drinketh in the Dews, and Rain of Heaven, *which brings forth briars and thorns, which is rejected, and nigh unto cursing, whose end is to be burnt.* Heb. vi. 4, 5, 6, 7, 8.

When Men obstinately resist the perpetual Motions and Sollicitations of the Holy Spirit, he withdraws from them, and gives them up to their own Counsels, as we leave off persuading those who will **not** be persuaded.

And

And when the Spirit of God forsakes such Men, the evil Spirit seizeth them, that Spirit which ruleth in the Children of Disobedience, *Eph.* ii. 3. For the World is divided into the Kingdom of Darkness and the Kingdom of Light, *Col.* i. 13. and those who are not under the Government of the divine Spirit, *are led captive by the Devil at his will,* 2 *Tim.* ii. 6. and therefore our Saviour hath taught us to pray to be delivered from Evil, ἀπό τȣ̃ πονηρȣ̃, from the evil One; that is, from the Devil: For that is a hopeless State, when God gives us up to the Government of evil Spirits: Nay when Men harden themselves in Sin, they are rejected by the good Providence of God, which secures good Men from, or delivers them out of, Temptation, as our Saviour has taught us to pray, *Lead us not into temptation;* as a Father keeps a watchful Eye over a dutiful Child, to preserve him from any Harm, and to chuse the most proper Condition and Circumstances of Life for him, but suffers a Prodigal to go where he pleases, and undo himself as fast as he can. And whoever considers the Weakness and Folly of human Nature, and the Power of Temptations, must needs conclude that Man given up to Ruin, who is rejected by the good Spirit of God, and cast out of the Care of his Providence.

Into this miserable State Men may bring themselves by Sin, who though it does not make them uncapable of Mercy, if they do repent, yet it makes it morally impossible that they should repent. It is this the Apostle to the *Hebrews* warns them against, from the Example of the Hardness and Infidelity of the *Israelites* in the Wilderness, of whom God sware, *that they shall not enter into his rest*; as appears from the Application he himself makes of it, Heb. iii. 12, 13. *Take heed, brethren, lest there be in any of you an evil heart of unbelief, in departing from the living God: But exhort one another daily, while it is called to-day, lest any of you be hardened through the deceitfulness of sin.*

This is a plain Account of that great Question, concerning the Length of the Day of Grace. Men may out-live the Time of Repentance, may so harden themselves in Sin, as to make their Repentance morally impossible; but they cannot out-live the Mercies of God to true Penitents. This is Reason enough to discourage Men from delaying their Repentance, and indulging themselves in a vicious Course of Life, *Lest they should be hardened, by the deceitfulness of sin*, and should be forsaken by God: But it is no Reason to discourage true Penitents from trusting in the Mercy of God, how late soever their Repentance be; for while we live in this World, the Door of Grace and Mercy is not shut against true Penitents.

3. But

3. But yet the Reasons of lengthning the Day of Grace and Mercy, do not reach beyond this Life. This sufficiently appears from what I have already said; and for a further Confirmation of it, I shall add but this one comprehensive Reason, *viz.* That the Grace of the Gospel is confined to the Church on Earth; and therefore this Life is the only Time to obtain the Remission of our Sins, and a Title to future Glory. We shall be finally absolved from all our Sins, and rewarded with eternal Life at the Day of Judgment; but we must sue out our Pardon, and make our Calling and Election sure in this World.

The Gospel of Christ, which is the Gospel of Grace, and contains the Promises of Pardon and immortal Life, is preached only to Men on Earth, and concerns none else.

For this Reason Christ became Man, cloathed with Flesh and Blood as we are, that he might be the Saviour of Mankind; which he need not have done, had not their Salvation been to be wrought in this World: For could they have been saved in the next, his Grace might have met them soon enough there. And therefore, at the Birth of our Saviour, the Angels sang, *Glory be to God in the highest, on earth peace, good will towards men,* Luke ii. 14.

The Sacrifice of Christ upon the Cross (as all *Jewish* Sacrifices, which were Types of the Sacrifice

Sacrifice of the Cross were) was offered for the Expiation of the Sins of living Men, or at least considered as living, not of the dead.

He carried his Blood into Heaven (as the High-Priest did the Blood of the Sacrifice into the Holy of Holies) there to make Expiation, and to intercede for us; but this Intercession, though made in Heaven, relates only to Men on Earth, as his Sacrifice did. The earthly Tabernacle was a Type of the Church on Earth; and that only, and the Worshippers in it, were expiated by Sacrifices.

There are two Sacraments whereby the Grace of the Gospel is applied to us, and which are the ordinary Means of Salvation, Baptism and the Lord's Supper; and they are confined to the Church on Earth; and if they have not their Effect here, they cannot have it in the next World. These unite us to Christ as Members of his Body; and then the Holy Spirit, which animates the Body of Christ, takes Possession of us, renews and sanctifies us; but if we prove dead and barren Branches in this spiritual Vine; if the Censures of the Church do not cut us off from the Body of Christ, Death will; and then we can never be re-united to him, nor saved by him in the next World. Faith in Christ, and Repentance from dead Works, are the great Gospel Terms of Pardon and Salvation, and these are confined to this World: There may be something like them in the next World; such a

Faith

Faith as makes the Devils tremble; such Repentance as is nothing else but despairing Agonies, and a hopeless and tormenting Remorse: But such a Faith as purifies the Heart, as conquers this present World, as brings forth the Fruits of Righteousness; such a Repentance as reforms our Lives, as undoes all our past Sins, as redresses the Injuries we have done to our Neighbours, and the Scandal we have given to the World; such a Faith, and such a Repentance, which alone are the true Christian Graces of Faith and Repentance, are proper only for this Life, and can be exercised only in this Life, while we have this World to conquer, and the Flesh to subdue to the Spirit, while we can restore our ill-gotten Riches, and set a visible Example of Piety and Virtue.

From hence it is very evident, that no Man who dies in a State of Sin and Impenitence, can be saved by Christ, and by the Grace of the Gospel in the next World; for the whole Ministration of Gospel-Grace is confined to this Life; and if they cannot be saved by Christ, I know no other Name whereby they can be saved: And thus Death puts an End to all the flattering Hopes of Sinners.

3. Now if this Life be only our State of Trial and Probation for Eternity; if Death puts a final End to our Day of Grace and Time of Working, then Death must translate us to an immutable and unchangeable State.

By

By this I do not mean, that as soon as we go out of these Bodies, our Souls will immediately be as happy or miserable as ever they shall be; the perfect Rewards of good Men are reserved for the Day of Judgment, as the final Punishments of bad Men are; when our Lord *shall say to those on his right hand, Come ye blessed of my Father, inherit the kingdom prepared for you from the foundation of the world:* And *to them on the left hand, Go ye cursed into everlasting fire, prepared for the devil and his angels,* Matth. xxv. 34, 41.

But tho' the Happiness or Miseries of the next World may increase, yet the State can never alter; that is, if we die in a State of Grace and Favour with God, we shall always continue so; if we die in a State of Sin, under the Wrath and Displeasure of God, there is no altering our State in the other World, we must abide under his Wrath for ever. This is the necessary Consequence of what I have already said, which all aimed at this Point, that *once dying* puts us to an immutable and unchangeable State; and therefore I shall wave any farther Proof of this, and only desire you seriously to consider of it.

1. Now first, since Death puts an end to our Day of Grace, and determines our final State for ever, and this Death comes but once, all Men must confess of what mighty Consequence it is to die well, that Death may find us well disposed, and well prepared for
another

another World. Men use their utmost Prudence and Caution in doing that which can be done but once for their whole Lives, especially if the Happiness of their whole Lives depends on it; for no Error can be corrected in what is to be done but once; and certainly we have much more Reason to prepare to die once; which translates us to an immutable State of Happiness or Misery. This ought to be the Work and Business of our whole Lives, to prepare for Death, which comes but *once*, but that *once* is for Eternity. What unpardonable Folly is it, for any Man to be surprized by Death! To fall into the Grave without thinking of it! To commit a Mistake, which may be retrieved again, to be guilty of some Neglect and Inadvertency, when the Hurt we suffer by it may be repaired by future Diligence and Caution, is much more excusable, because it is not so fatal and irreparable Folly: In this Case Experience may teach Wisdom, and Wisdom is a good Purchase though we may pay dear for it; but a wise Man will use great Caution in making an Experiment, which if it fail will cost him his Life, because that can never be tried a second Time; and Experience is of no Use in such Things as can be done but once.

And this is the Case of dying; we can die but once, and if we miscarry that once we are undone for ever: And what considering

Man would make such dangerous Experiments as Sinners do every Day, when their Souls are the Price of the Experiment! Who would try how long Death will delay his coming? How long he may sin on safely without thinking of Death or Judgment? Whether Death will give him timely Notice to repent? Or whether God will give him Grace to repent if he does? Who would venture the infinite Hazards of a Death-bed Repentance? Whether after a long Life of Sin and Wickedness, a few distracted, confused, and almost despairing Sighs and Groans will carry him to Heaven? If such bold Adventurers as these, when they have discovered their Mistake and Folly, could return back into this World, and live over their Lives again, the Hazard were not so great; but this is an Experiment not to be twice made. If they sin on 'till they harden themselves in Sin, and are forsaken of the Grace of God; if Death comes long before they expected, and cuts them off by Surprize, and without Warning; if their dying and despairing Agonies and Horrors should not prove a truly godly Sorrow, *not that repentance to salvation never to be repented of*, they are lost to Eternity. And what wise Man would expose his Soul to such Hazard as this? Who would not take care to make his Calling and Election sure before Death comes; and in a Matter of such infinite Concernment, wherein one Miscarriage

age is irreparable, to prevent Danger at a Distance?

2. We hence learn how necessary it is for those who begin well to persevere unto the End: It is the Conclusion of our Lives which determines our future State; as God expressly tells us by his Prophet *Ezekiel*, Ezek. xviii. 21, 24. *If the wicked will turn from all his sins that he hath committed, and keep my statutes, and do that which is lawful and right, he shall surely live, he shall not die: All his transgressions that he hath committed, they shall not be mentioned unto him; in his righteousness that he hath done, he shall live.* —— *But when the righteous turneth away from his righteousness, and committeth iniquity, and doth according to all the abominations that the wicked man doth, shall he live? All the righteousness that he hath done shall not be mentioned; in his trespass that he hath trespassed, and in his sin that he hath sinned, in them shall he die.* And throughout the *New Testament*, the Reward is promised only to those who continue to the End. And what I have now discoursed, gives a plain Account of this; for our whole Life is a State of Trial and Probation; and if we leave off before our Work be done, if we stop or run backwards before we come to the End of our Race, we must lose our Reward, our Crown. The Christian Life is a State of Warfare, and we know the last Battle gives the final Conquest: And this cannot be otherwise:

therwise; because what comes last, undoes what went before. When a wicked Man turns from his Wickedness, and does good, God in infinite Mercy, through the Merits and Mediation of Christ, will forgive his Sins, because he has put them away from him, and undone them by Repentance and a new Life.

When a righteous Man turns from his Righteousness, and does wickedly, his Righteousness shall be forgotten, because he has renounced it, and parted with it, and is a righteous Man no longer. Now when God comes to judge the World, he will judge Men as he then finds them; he will not enquire what they have been, but what they are; he will not condemn a righteous Man, because he has been wicked; nor justify a wicked Man, because he has been righteous: For this would be to punish the Righteous, and to reward the Wicked. Such as we are when we die, such we shall continue for ever; and therefore it is the last Scene of our Lives which determines our future State.

And should not this make us very jealous and watchful over ourselves? *To take heed lest there be in any of us an evil heart* Heb. iii. 12. *of unbelief, in departing from the living God. Looking diligently, lest any Man fail of the grace of God; lest any root of bitterness springing up, trouble* Heb. xii. 15. *you, and thereby many be defiled;* lest *after we have escaped the pollutions*

tions of the world, through the knowledge of the Lord and Saviour Jesus Christ, we are again entangled therein, and overcome, and it happen to us according to the true proverb, The dog is returned to his vomit again, and the sow that was washed, to her wallowing in the mire. This, as the Apostle tells us, *makes our latter end worse than the beginning; for it had been better for us not to have known the way of righteousness, than after we have known it, to turn from the holy commandment delivered to us.* 2 Pet. ii. 20, 21, 22.

Let those consider this, who have been blessed with a religious Education, and trained up in the Exercises of Piety and Virtue; who have preserved themselves from the Pollutions of youthful Lusts, and spent their vigorous Age in the Service of God; can you be contented to lose all these hopeful Beginnings; to lose all your Triumphs and Victories over the World and the Flesh? When you have out-rid all the Storms and Hurricanes of a tempting World for so many Years, will you suffer yourselves to be ship-wrecked in the Haven? When you are come within View of the promised Land, will you suffer your Hearts then to fail you? Will you then murmur and rebel against God, and die in the Wilderness?

There has been a very warm Dispute about the Perseverance of Saints; whether those who are once in a State of Grace, shall al-

ways

ways continue so? I will not undertake to decide this Controversy; but thus much I will say, (and that I think is all that is needful for a Christian to know about it:) That to be in a State of Grace, is to have an inward Principle of Holiness, which brings forth the Fruit of a holy Life; then to persevere in a State of Grace, is to persevere in the Practice of Holiness and Virtue; that many who have begun well, and have thought themselves, and have been thought by others, to be truly good Men, have afterwards been overcome by the Temptations of the World, and defiled themselves with the impure Lusts of it; that if such Men ever were good Men, and in a State of Grace, they fall from Grace when they forsake the Paths of Holiness; and that those, who do thus fall away, who after promising Beginnings, do all the Abominations of the Wicked, and live and die in such a State, shall never enter into Heaven. We shall receive our final Doom and Sentence, according to that State and Condition in which Death finds us. What is said upon another Account, That we must call no Man happy before Death, is true in this Sense; no Man is a Conqueror, but he who dies so: Those Men deceive themselves, who confidently pretend to be still in a State of Grace and Favour with God, because formerly they were good Men, though now they are grown very bad. This is to persevere in a State of

Favour

Favour with God, without persevering in Holiness, which overthrows the Gospel of our Saviour, and will miserably deceive those Men who have no better Foundation for their Hopes.

3. We hence learn how dangerous it is to die in the actual Commission of any known and wilful Sin: Such Men go into the other World, and go to Judgment with actual Guilt upon them, they die in their Sins; for they could not repent of them before they died, because they died in the Commission of them, and there is no Repentance, and therefore no Pardon in the next World. This has been, and very often is, the miserable, and, I fear, the hopeless State of a great many Sinners. How many are there, who not only drink themselves into a Fever, which takes some Time to kill them, and gives them some Time to repent of their Sins, and to ask God's Pardon; but drink themselves dead, or, which is much at one, as to this Case, drink away their Reason and Senses, and then fall from their Horses, or down a Precipice, and perish by some evil Accident; or when they are inflamed with Wine forget their old Friendships, and fall by each other's Hands? How many others have perished in the very Act of Adultery, or, which is much the same, in quarrelling for a Strumpet, in the Rage and Fury of Lust? How many die in the very Act of Theft and Robbery? All such

Men receive the prefent Punifhment of their Sins in this World, and carry the unrepented Guilt of them into the next; and if Men fhall be damned who die in their Sins without Repentance, fuch Mens Condition is defperate. And this may be the Cafe of any Man who ventures upon a wilful Sin; he may die in the very Act of it, and then his Repentance will come too late in the next World: And this fo often happens, that no wife Man would venture his Soul upon it.

But there are two Sins efpecially, which this Confideration fhould deter Men from, *viz.* Duelling, and Self-murder.

When Men have fuch a Refentment of Affronts and Injuries, as to revenge themfelves with their Swords, and either to thirft after each other's Blood, or at leaft to ftake their Lives, and to venture killing, or being killed, to decide the Quarrel; thefe Men have the Hearts of Murtherers, who would kill if they could, or at leaft would venture killing their Brother, to appeafe their Refentments or Revenge, which is a mortal and murdering Revenge, whether it murder or not; and therefore if fuch Men fall in the Quarrel, as many do, without Time to afk God's Pardon with their laft Breath, they die under the Guilt of Murder unrepented of; though they do not kill, but are killed, yet they die with murderous Intentions, with a mortal Hatred and Revenge, for they would have

killed

killed if they could: And St. *John* tells us, *He that hateth his brother, is a murderer; and we know that no murderer hath eternal life abiding in him,* 1 John iii. 15. So that thefe Duellers do not only venture their Lives, but their Souls too, if they fall in the Quarrel; and how little foever they value their Lives, it is a little too much to pawn their Souls upon a Point of Honour.

As for Self-murder, if we will allow it to be a Sin, it is certain that no Man who commits it, can repent of it in this World, and there is no Pardon for Sins in the next World, which are not repented of in this. And yet why we fhould not think it as great a Sin to murder ourfelves, as to murder our Brother, I cannot imagine, for it has all the Marks of a very great Sin upon it.

It is as much Murder to kill ourfelves, as it is to kill another Man; and therefore it is a Breach of the fixth Commandment, *Thou fhalt not kill.* The Reafon againft Murder is the fame; *For in the image of God made he man,* Gen. ix. 6. And he who kills himfelf, deftroys God's Image, as much as he who kills another Man. The more unnatural the Sin is, or the greater Obligations we have to preferve the Life of the Perfon whom we kill, the greater the Sin is. To murder a kind Friend and Benefactor, is a greater Evil than to murder a Stranger: To murder a Parent, or a Child, a Wife, or a Hufband, is

Q 3   ftill

still a greater Evil, because they are so much nearer ourselves; and if the Nearness of the Relation increases the Sin, no Body is so near to us as ourselves, and therefore there is no such unnatural Murder as this.

The Excuses which are made for Self-murder, will not justify the Murder of any other Man in the World. Though we should see a Friend, whom we love like ourselves, labouring under intolerable Pains, or insupportable Misfortunes and Calamities of Life, tho' he should importune and beseech us to put an end to his Suffering, by putting an end to a miserable Life; though out of great Kindness and Compassion we heartily desire to follow him to his Grave, yet we must not kill him; neither the Laws of God nor Man will allow this. And yet if Self-love be the Measure of our Love to other Men, and will justify Self-murder, when we are grown weary of Life, when we either despise the World, or think it best to make our Escape out of it; I cannot imagine why we may not do the same Kindness for a Friend or Brother, when he desires it, as we may do for ourselves: The Reason is the same in both; and if it will not justify both, it can justify neither.

For there is no Foundation that I know of for what some pretend, that God has given us greater Power over our own Lives, than over other Mens. We find no such Power given us in Scripture, which is the only Revelation

velation of God's Will; and I am sure Nature teaches us no such Thing; nay, Nature teaches the quite contrary. The natural Aversion to Death, and the natural Principle of Self-preservation, were not only intended to make us cautious of any Hurt or Mischief which other Men may do us, but to make us careful to do no Hurt to, much less to destroy, ourselves; and therefore the Voice of Nature is, That we must preserve our own Lives and Beings.

When God made us, he did not make us the absolute Lords and Masters of ourselves; we cannot dispose of ourselves as we please, but are his Creatures and Subjects, and must receive Laws from him; and that in such Instances wherein the Injury is done only to ourselves. We must not abuse our own Bodies by Intemperance, and Luxury, or Lust, though neither the Publick, nor any private Persons are injured by it: And if we have not Power over our own Bodies in lesser Instances, much less to kill them.

And if it be a Sin to destroy our own Lives, it is the most mortal and damning Sin, for it destroys Soul and Body together, because it makes our Repentance impossible; unless Men can repent of their Sin, and obtain God's Pardon for it, before they have committed it, or can repent and obtain their Pardon in the next World. Did Men seriously consider this, it is impossible that the greatest Shame and Infamy,

Infamy, Want or Suffering, or whatever it is that makes them weary of Life, should be thought so intolerable, as to make them force their Passage into the other World to escape it, when such a violent and unnatural Escape will cost them their Souls. Men may be in such evil Circumstances as may make Death desirable; but no considering Man will exchange the Sufferings of this Life for the endless Miseries of the next. If we cannot destroy our Lives, and put an end to our present Sufferings, without destroying our Souls too, we must be contented to live on, and bear our Lot patiently in this World; which, whatever it is, is much more easy and tolerable than to be eternally miserable.

And yet God forbid that I should pronounce a final and peremptory Sentence upon all those unfortunate Persons who have died by their own Hands. We know not what Allowances God may make for some Mens Opinions of the Lawfulness of it, and for the Distraction of other Mens Thoughts and Passions, through a settled Melancholy, or some violent Temptation: My Business is not to limit the sovereign and prerogative Grace of God, but to declare the Nature of the Thing according to the Terms of the Gospel. To murder ourselves, is the most unnatural Murder: It is a damning Sin, and such a Sin as no Man can repent of in this World; and therefore unless God forgive it without Repentance,

pentance, it can never be forgiven; and the Gospel of Christ gives us no Commission to preach Forgiveness of Sin without Repentance. The Gospel-Grace, which only forgives Penitents, cannot save such Men; and he is a very bold Man, and ventures very far upon unpromised and uncovenanted Mercy, who will commit a Sin which the Grace of the Gospel cannot pardon.

All that I have to add under this Head, is the Case of those who die in Despair of God's Mercy. This is commonly thought a very hopeless State; for to despair of the Mercy of God is a great Sin, and therefore such Men die in the actual Commission of Sin unrepented of, and By-standers are apt to suspect their Despair to be little better than their final Doom and Sentence. And yet many times we see Men labouring under Despair in their last Agonies, who have, to all outward Appearance, lived very innocent and virtuous Lives; and it is hard to judge so severely of them, as to think they were secret Hypocrites, and that God has finally rejected them, because they pass such a severe Judgment upon themselves.

Now, I confess, Despair is as uncomfortable a State as any Man can die in; but I cannot think it so fatal and dangerous as some imagine; for let us consider what the Nature of Despair is, and wherein the Sinfulness of it consists.

To

To disbelieve the Promises of Grace and Mercy, made to true penitent Sinners by Jesus Christ, is Infidelity, not Despair; and this indeed is a great and unpardonable Sin; for it is to renounce the Faith of Christ, and the Grace of the Gospel. But this is not what we commonly call Despair. Some Men believe the Gospel of Christ, and all the Promises of it, as firmly as others do: They do not doubt but God will forgive all true Penitents, through the Merits and Mediation of Jesus Christ; and therefore are as true and sincere Believers as those who do not despair; but their Despair is in the Application of these Promises to themselves. That is, they fear that they are not within the Terms and Conditions of Gospel-Grace; that they are not true Penitents; that their Day of Grace is expired, and now they shall not receive the Blessing, though, as *Esau* did, they seek it earnestly with Tears; or, it may be, that they are Reprobates, who have no Right to the Promises of the Gospel.

Now if these Men may upon all other Accounts be very good Christians, but are either oppressed with Melancholy, or disturbed with false and mistaken Notions of Religion; can we think that their Melancholy or Mistakes, which makes them pass so false a Judgment upon themselves, shall make God condemn them too, who knows them better than they know themselves? Should a Man who has a

delirious

delirious Fancy, accuse himself of Theft, or Murder, or Treason, which he was never guilty of; would a just and righteous Judge, who certainly knows that he is not guilty of these Crimes, condemn him, only because he condemns himself? Suppose a Man who is in the right Way to Heaven, should be persuaded by some Travellers he meets, that he has mistaken his Way; and upon this he should fall into great Horrors and Agonies, and give himself for lost; is this Man ever the farther off of Heaven because he is persuaded that he has mistaken his Way?

The false Judgments dying Men make of themselves, either through Enthusiasm, Presumption, or Despair, shall not determine their final State. Men may go to Hell with all the Triumphs of a deluded Fancy, which promises nothing less than eternal Glories; and those who go trembling out of this World, may find themselves happily mistaken in the next. It is a wrong Notion of justifying Faith, which makes Men conclude Despair to be so damning and unpardonable a Sin. If justifying Faith were nothing else but a strong Belief and Persuasion that we are justified, that were good Reason to conclude Despair to be a mortal Sin, because it is a direct Contradiction to justifying Faith: Nay, if the justifying Act of Faith were an actual Reliance and Recumbency on Christ for Salvation, Despair must be very mortal; because

cause while Men are under those Agonies, they do not, they cannot, rely on Christ for Salvation; for they believe that Christ has cast them off, and will not save them. But if to believe in Christ, that he is the Saviour of the World, that he has made Expiation for our Sins, and intercedes for us at the Right Hand of God, and is able to save to the uttermost all those that come unto God by him; that he will save all true penitent Sinners, and will save us, if we be true Penitents; I say, if such a Faith as this, when it brings forth the genuine Fruits of Repentance and a holy Life, be a true justifying Faith, this is consistent with the blackest Despair, and then Men may be in a justified State, though they are never so strongly persuaded that they are Reprobates. A very good Man may have his Fancy disturbed, and may pass a false Judgment upon himself; but this is no Reason for God to condemn him, no more than God will justify a presuming and enthusiastick Hypocrite, because he justifies himself.

3. If Death puts a final End to our Work, and Labour, and shuts up our Accounts, then it concerns us to do all the Good that we can while we live. *Whatever our hand findeth to do, we should do it with all our might, seeing there is no wisdom, nor knowledge, nor working in the grave, whither we are hasting.* Not that the next World is an idle and unactive State,

State, where we shall know nothing, and have nothing to do; but Death puts an end to our working for the other World: Nothing can be brought to our Account at the Day of Judgment, but the Good we do while we live here: For this only we shall receive our Reward proportionable to the Increase and wise Improvement of our Talents.

And is not this a good Reason why we should begin to serve God betimes, and take all Opportunities of doing Good, since we have only a short Life to work for Eternity? There are great and glorious Rewards prepared for good Men; but those shall have the brightest Crowns, who do the most Good in the World; who *are rich in good works, and lay up for themselves treasures in heaven.*

Indeed, the meanest Place in Heaven is a Happiness too great for us to conceive, I am sure much greater than our greatest Deserts; but since our bountiful Lord will reward all the good Service we do, why should we neglect to do any Good, when such Neglects will lessen our Reward? Why should we be contented to lose any Degrees of Glory? This is a holy Ambition, to be as good, and to be as happy, as God can make us.

This is never thought of by those Men who have no greater Designs than to escape Hell; but as for the Glories of Heaven, they can be contented with the least Share of them. No Man will ever get to Heaven, who so despises

spises the Glories of it: And if a late Repentance should open our Eyes not only to see our Sins, but to alter our Opinions of this World and of the next, yet we can never recal our past Time; and that little Time that remains, which is the very Dregs and Sediment of our Lives, the dead and unactive Scene, will minister very few Opportunities of doing Good; and if it did, we are capable of doing very little; and if we get to Heaven, that will be all; but the bright and triumphant Crowns shall be bestowed upon those who have improved their Time and their Talents better.

It is the Good we do while we live, that shall be rewarded; and therefore we must take care to do Good while we live. It is well when Men, who do no Good while they live, will remember to do some Good when they die. But if God should accept such Presents as these, yet it will make great Abatements in the Account, that they kept their Riches themselves as long as they could, and would part with nothing to God, 'till they could keep it no longer. It is not the Gift, but the Mind of the Giver that is accepted. Under the Gospel, God is pleased with a living Sacrifice; but the Offerings of the Dead (and such these testamentary Charities are, which are intended to have no Effect as long as we live) are no better than dead Sacrifices; and it may be questioned whether they will be brought into the

the Account of our Lives, if we do no Good while we live. The Case is different as to those who did all the Good they could while they lived, and when they saw they could live no longer, took care to do Good after Death. Such surviving Charities as these prolong our Lives, and add daily to our Account; when such Men are removed into the other World, they are doing Good in this World still, they have a Stock a going below, the Increase and Improvements of which will follow them into the other World. Men who have been charitable all their Lives, may prolong their Charity after Death; and this will be brought to the Account of their Lives: But I cannot see, how a Charity which commences after Death, can be called doing Good while we live; and then it cannot belong to the Account of our Lives. All that can be said for it is this; That they make their Wills, whereby they bequeath these Charities while they live; and therefore their bequeathing these Charities is an Act of their Lives; but they never intend they shall take place while they live, but after their Death. And when they never intend their Charity to be an Act of their Lives, I know not why God should account it so. These Death-bed Charities are too like a Death-bed Repentance: Men seem to give their Estates to God and the Poor, just as they part with their Sins, when they can keep them no longer.

ger. This is much such a Charity, as it is Devotion to bequeath our dead Bodies to the Church or Chancel, which we should never visit while we lived.

But yet, as I have already intimated, this is the only Way to prolong our Lives, and to have an increasing Account after Death, to lay the Foundations of some great Good to the World, which shall outlive us: Which like Seed sown in the Earth, shall spring up, and yield a plentiful Harvest, while we sleep sweetly in the Dust. Such as the religious Education of our Children and Families, which may propagate itself in the World, and last many Ages after we are dead; the Endowment of publick Schools and Hospitals; in a word, whatever is for the Relief of the Necessitous, or for the Instruction and good Government of Mankind, when we are gone. To do Good while we live, and to lay Designs of great Good to future Generations, will both come into our Account, and this may extend the Account of our Lives, much beyond the short Period of them in this World.

5. If Death puts an end to our Account, methinks a dying Bed is a little of the latest to begin it; for this is to begin just where we must end. The Account of our Lives is the Account of the Good or Evil we have done while we lived: And what Account can a dying Man give of this, who has spent his whole Life in Sin and Wickedness? If he must be

be judged according to what he hath done in the Body, how sad is his Account; and how impossible is it for him to mend it now? For when he is just a dying, it is too late for him to begin to live: If *without holiness no man shall see God,* How hopeless is his Condition, who has lived a wicked and profligate Life all his Days; and is now past living, and therefore past living a holy Life? A Man who is confined to a sick and dying Bed, is uncapable of exercising the Virtues of Life: His Time of Work is over, almost as perfectly over as if he were dead; and therefore his Account is finished, and he must expect his Reward according to what he has already done.

No, you'll say, he may still repent of his Sins; and a true Penitent shall find Mercy even at his last Gasp. Now I readily grant, that all true Penitents shall be saved, whensoever they truly repent; but it is hard to think, that any dying Sorrows, or the dying Vows and Resolutions of Sinners, shall be accepted by GOD for true Repentance: The Mistakes of this Matter are very fatal, and therefore I shall briefly explain it.

In expounding the Promises of the Gospel, we must take care to reconcile the Gospel to itself, and not make one Part of it contradict or overthrow another. Now, as the Gospel promises Pardon of Sin to true Repentance,

tance, so it makes Holiness of Life as necessary a Condition of Salvation, as
true Repentance. *Without holiness
no man shall see* GOD. *GOD will render to
every man according to his deeds: To
them who by patient continuance in
well doing, seek for glory, and honour, and immortality, eternal life; but unto
them that are contentious, and do not obey the
truth, but obey unrighteousness, indignation and
wrath, tribulation and anguish upon every soul
of man that doeth evil;——but glory, honour,
and peace to every man that worketh good. Be
not deceived,* GOD *is not mocked;
for whatsoever a man soweth, that
shall he also reap: For he that soweth to the
flesh, shall of the flesh reap corruption; but he
that soweth to the spirit, shall of the spirit
reap life everlasting.* The Promises of Forgiveness to Repentance, are not more express
than these Texts are, which declare that we
shall be rewarded according to our Works:
And we have as much Reason to believe the
one as the other; and if we believe the Gospel, we must believe them both: And then
Repentance and a holy Life are both necessary
to Salvation: And then the dying Sorrows of
Sinners, who have lived very wicked Lives,
and are past mending them now, cannot be
true saving Repentance. If Sorrow for Sin
without a holy Life can carry Men to Heaven, then I am sure Holiness is not necessary;

then

Heb. xii. 14.

Rom. ii. 6, 7,
8, 9, 10.

Gal. vi. 7, 8.

then Men may see God without Holiness, and then the Promises of Pardon to Repentance (if this dying Sorrow be true Repentance) overthrows the Necessity of a holy Life; and the Necessity of a holy Life contradicts the Promises of Pardon to such Penitents; and then either one or both of them must be false.

To state this Matter plainly, and in a few Words, we must distinguish between two Kinds of Repentance: 1. The Baptismal Repentance: 2. Repentance upon a Relapse, or falling into any known and wilful Sin.

I. By Baptismal Repentance, I mean that Repentance which is necessary in adult Persons, in order to their receiving Christian Baptism: This is the Repentance which is most frequently mention'd in the *New Testament*, and to which the Promise of Remission and Forgiveness is annexed: This our Saviour preached, *Repent, for the Kingdom of heaven is at hand*, Matth. iv. 17. This he gave Authority to his Apostles to preach, *that repentance and remission of sins should be preached in his name among all nations*, Luke xxiv. 47. Now this Repentance, both as to *Jews* and *Heathens*, who embraced the Faith of Christ, was renouncing all their former Sins, and false, superstitious, or idolatrous Worship; and this qualified them for Baptism, in which they obtained the Remission of all their Sins in the Name of Chrift. And for this Reaſon Remiſſion of Sins is promis'd to Repentance; becauſe all ſuch Penitents are received to Baptiſm, which is the waſhing of Regeneration, which waſhes away all their Sins, and puts them into a State of Grace and Favour with God; as St. *Peter* tells the *Jews, Repent, and be baptized very one of you in the name of Jeſus Chriſt, for the remiſſion of ſins,* Acts ii. 38. And much to the ſame Purpoſe *Ananias* told St. *Paul, Paul, Ariſe, and be baptized, and waſh away thy ſins, calling on the name of the Lord,* Acts xxii. 16. And I know not any one Text in the *New Teſtament*, wherein the Remiſſion of Sins is abſolutely promiſed to Repentance; but what muſt be underſtood of this Baptiſmal Repentance: And then Repentance, and Remiſſion of Sins are inſeparably annexed; becauſe ſuch Penitents waſh away all their Sins in Baptiſm; and come pure and undefiled out of that myſtical Fountain, which is ſet open for Sin and for Uncleanneſs to waſh in, and to be clean.

Now I grant, ſhould any Perſon who comes to Baptiſm rightly qualified and diſpoſed, with a ſincere Repentance, and ſtedfaſt Faith in Chriſt, die ſoon after he is baptized, before he has Time and Opportunity to exerciſe any of the Graces of the Chriſtian Life; ſuch a Man ſhall go to Heaven without actual Holineſs: The Remiſſion of his Sins in Baptiſm, upon his Repentance, will ſave him; though he he have not Time to bring forth the Fruits of Repentance in a holy Life: And this is the only Case I know of, wherein a Penitent can be saved without actual Holiness; *viz.* by Baptismal Grace and Regeneration. Only the Primitive Church, and I think with very good Reason, allowed the same to Martyrdom, when it prevented the Baptism of young Converts; as we know under the Pagan Persecutions, young Converts who made bold Confessions of their Faith in Christ, were hurried away to Martyrdom, before they had Opportunity of being baptized: But such Men were baptized in their own Blood; and that supplied the want of Water-Baptism, which they could not have. Now in this Case also, if Martyrdom be instead of Baptism, as the Primitive Church thought it; then had any Heathen been converted from a lewd and profligate Life to the Faith of Christ, and been immediately apprehended and halled to Martyrdom, before he could be either baptized, or give any other Testimony of the Reformation of his Life and Manners, but by dying a Martyr; this Man also would go to Heaven without actual Holiness of Life; as a baptized Penitent, who dies immediately after his Baptism, shall.

And this seems to me to give the best Account of the Case of the penitent Thief upon the Cross; which one Example has encouraged so many Sinners to delay their Repent-tance to the laſt Minute, and has deſtroyed ſo many Souls by ſuch Delays. His Caſe ſeems to be this: It is probable he had heard of Chriſt, and the Fame of his great Miracles before, and that Opinion ſome had of him, that he was that *Meſſias* whom God had promiſed to ſend into the World; for we can hardly think that any Man who lived in thoſe Days, ſhould never have heard of Chriſt, whoſe Fame went thro' the whole Nation: But yet the Courſe of Life this Thief led, gave him no great Curioſity to enquire into ſuch Matters, till he was apprehended for Robbery, and condemned to die at the ſame Time with Chriſt; this extraordinary Accident made him more curiouſly enquire after him, and learn all the Circumſtances of his Apprehenſion, and Trial, and Uſage, and Behaviour, and Anſwers, eſpecially when he ſaw him, and was to die with him; and in ſhort, he obſerved ſo much as convinced him, that he was the true *Meſſias*, thoʹ he ſaw him nailed in ſo ſhameful a manner to the Croſs.

Now if this was his Caſe, and we muſt ſuppoſe this or ſomething like it, unleſs we will ſay that he was miraculouſly inſpired upon the Croſs with the Faith of Chriſt, without knowing any thing of him before, which has no Foundation in the Story, and is without any Precedent or Example; I ſay, if this was his Caſe, according to the Principles laid down, we muſt grant, that if this Thief had re-

nounced

nounced his wicked Course of Life, and professed his Faith in Christ, and been baptized in his Name, tho' he had immediately suffered upon the Cross, he must have gone directly to Heaven or Paradise, as Christ promised him he should, by Virtue of Remission of all his Sins in Baptism: Nay, we must grant farther, that if instead of Baptism, he had at that Time died a Martyr for the Profession of his Faith in Christ; this would have supplied the Place of Baptism, and have translated him into Paradise: All then that we have to enquire is, whether this Confession of Christ upon the Cross, might not as well supply the Want of Water-Baptism, as Martyrdom: Nay, whether it were not equivalent to Martyrdom itself, and might not reasonably be accepted by our Saviour as such. Water-Baptism he could not have, a Martyr he could not die, for he died a Malefactor; but he confessed his Faith in Christ, when he saw him hanging upon the Cross, which was a more glorious Act of Faith, than to have died upon the Cross for him. He confessed Christ when his own Disciples fled from him, and when *Peter* himself denied him; and discovered his Glory through the meanest Disguise that ever it was concealed under, even in this World; and why should not this pass for the Faith and Confession of Martyrdom? And then the Thief upon the Cross was saved as by Baptism; which is, *Not the putting away*

away the filth of the flesh, but the answer of a good conscience towards GOD, 1 Pet. iii. 21. Which Description of Baptism gives us a plain Reason, why Martyrdom should supply the Place of Baptism, and is a good Reason, why the Thief's Confession of Christ upon the Cross should do so.

This Example then of the Thief upon the Cross, is no reasonable Encouragement to any baptized Christian to live a wicked Life, and delay his Repentance till the Hour of Death, in hopes of being saved at last, as he was; for he was saved as new repenting Converts are by Baptism; not as baptized Sinners hope to be, by a Death-bed Sorrow, and Remorse of Conscience.

And yet this is the only Example, which with any Shew of Reason is alledged to prove the Sufficiency of a Death-bed Repentance; for the Parable of the Labourers, who were called to work in the Vineyard at different Hours, some early in the Morning, others at the third, the sixth, the eleventh Hour of the Day, is nothing at all to this Purpose. The several Hours of the Day in that Parable, do not signify the several Hours of Mens Lives, but the different Ages of the World; and therefore those Labourers who are called into the Vineyard about the eleventh Hour of the World; that is, towards the End, or in the last Age of the World, might be called at the

Matth. xx. 1, &c.

Beginning

Beginning of their Lives, and work on to the End of them: For the Design of that Parable is to shew, that the *Gentiles*, who were called into the Vineyard, or received into the Church of Christ towards the Conclusion of the World, should be admitted to equal Privileges and Rewards with the *Jews*, who were God's ancient People, and had been called into the Vineyard, early in the Morning; which occasioned their murmuring against the good Man of the House; as we know the *Jews* murmured upon this Account; and nothing more prejudiced them against the Gospel of our Saviour, than that the *Gentiles* were received into the Church without Circumcision. The same thing our Saviour represents in the Parable of the Prodigal. The Return of the Prodigal to his Father's House, is the Conversion of the *Gentiles* who were the younger Brother, Luke xv. 13. &c. and had been a great Prodigal for many Ages; the elder Brother, who always lived at home with his Father, was the *Jewish* Church: But when this young Prodigal was received by his Father with Feasting and Musick, and all the Expressions of Joy, his elder Brother grew jealous of it, and thought himself much injured by his Father's Fondness of the returning Prodigal, and refused to come in, and bear his Part in the Solemnity; as the *Jews* rejected the Gospel, because the *Gentiles* were received into the Church.

And

And that this muſt be the true Meaning of the Parable of the Labourers, appears from this, That thoſe who were called into the Vineyard at the eleventh Hour, received a Reward equal to thoſe who had borne the Heat and Burden of the Day; which is agreeable enough, if we expound it of different Ages of the Church: For there is great Reaſon why the *Gentiles*, though they came later into the Vineyard, ſhould be made at leaſt equal with the *Jews*, who were God's ancient People; but if we expound this of entring into the Vineyard at different Ages of our Life, it ſeems very unequal, that thoſe who begin a Life of Virtue juſt at the Concluſion of their Lives, ſhould be equally rewarded with thoſe who have ſpent their whole Lives in the Service of God; that is, that thoſe who do very little Good, ſhall receive as great a Reward as thoſe who do a hundred times as much: Which is a direct Contradiction to the Scope and Deſign of our Saviour's Parables about the Pounds and Talents, *Matth.* xxv. 14, &c. *Luke* xix. 12, &c.

But ſuppoſe it were to be underſtood, not of the *Jewiſh* or Chriſtian Church, but of particular Chriſtians; yet their being called to work in the Vineyard, at what Hour ſoever it was, though the eleventh Hour, was their firſt Admiſſion into the Chriſtian Church, their firſt Converſion to the Faith of Chriſt; and from this Time they laboured in the Vineyard,

[...]ineyard, lived a holy and religious Life: [a]nd I readily grant, should a *Jew*, a *Turk*, [or] a *Pagan*, be converted to Christianity in the [e]venth Hour, in his declining Age, and [fr]om that Time live in Obedience to the [Go]spel of Christ; there is no doubt but he [sh]all be greatly rewarded: but what is this to [an]y of us, who were born of Christian [Pa]rents, baptized in our very Infancy, in[str]ucted in the Christian Religion from the [ver]y beginning, and have always professed [the] Faith of Christ, but lived like Pagans [an]d Infidels? We are not called into the [Vi]neyard at the eleventh Hour, but early in [the] Morning; and tho' Men who are called [at] the last Hour, shall be rewarded for that [Ho]ur's Work; this does not prove that Men, [wh]o entering into the Vineyard in the Morn[ing], play and riot away their Time 'till the [ele]venth Hour, shall receive a Day's Wages [for] an Hour's Work.

But suppose this too, yet it will not an[sw]er the Case of a Death-bed Repentance; [suc]h Men delay not 'till the eleventh Hour, [but] 'till Night comes, when they can do no [w]ork at all: Whereas those who came last [to] the Vineyard, wrought an Hour; now [tha]t God in infinite Grace and Goodness will [rew]ard Men for one Hour's Work, does not [pro]ve that he will reward those who do no [wo]rk, but spend their whole Day idly or wickedly,

wickedly, and only aſk his Pardon for not working at Night.

II. But what a fatal Cheat theſe Men put upon themſelves, will better appear, if we conſider the ſecond Kind of Repentance, which is Repentance after Baptiſm, when Men are relapſed into the Commiſſion of new Sins, after they have waſhed away all their old Sins in the Laver of Regeneration; which is the only Notion of Repentance concerned in this Queſtion: For ſuch Sinners when they come to die, are to repent of a whole Life ſpent in Wickedneſs, after Baptiſm; and this extremely alters the Caſe; for tho' Faith and Repentance, (as that Repentance ſignifies a Sorrow for paſt Sins, and the Purpoſes and Reſolutions of a new Life) be the only Conditions of baptiſmal Remiſſion and Juſtification, yet when we are baptized, we then covenant with God for an actual Obedience and Holineſs of Life; *To deny all ungodlineſs and worldly luſts, and to live ſoberly, righteouſly, and godlily in this preſent world:* And therefore mere Repentance, or a Sorrow for Sin, with the moſt ſolemn Reſolutions and Vows of a new Life (which is all the Repentance dying Men can have) cannot, according to the Terms of the Goſpel, be accepted inſtead of the Obedience and Holineſs of our Lives. Had the Goſpel ſaid, You ſhall either abſtain from all Sin, and do

good

od while you live, or repent of all your
is when you die; this had been a sufficient
icouragement for a Death-bed Repentance;
t when Holiness of Life is made the necessy Condition of seeing God, and
wrath of God is revealed from   Rom. i. 18.
ven against all unrighteousness and ungodliss of men; when we are so expressly foreirned, *That the unrighteous shall not inherit
: kingdom of God: be not deceived, neither
nicators, nor idolaters, nor adulers, nor effeminate, nor abusers of   1 Cor. vi.
mselves with mankind, nor thieves   9, 10.
r covetous, nor drunkards nor extortioners,
ill inherit the kingdom of God:* When our
viour expressly tells us, That it is only the
ers of the word are blessed*; that
every one that saith, Lord, Lord,*   Matt. xxvii. 1.
ll enter into the kingdom of hean, but he that doth the will of my Father
hich is in heaven; *that as for all others,
hat Pretences soever they make, *he will proIs to them, I never knew you; depart from
, ye that work iniquity:* I say whosoever after
r such express Declarations as these can persade himself, that Sorrow for Sin, and some
od Resolutions and fair Promises upon a
eath-bed, shall carry him to Heaven, tho'
has done no Good in his Life, and has
en guilty of all, or many of those Sins
hich the Gospel has threatned with Damnation,

nation, makes void the whole Gospel of our Saviour.

But you'll say, Is there no place then for Repentance under the Gospel? No Remission of Sins committed after Baptism? God forbid! For who then could be saved? Our Saviour has taught us to pray every Day, *Forgive us our trespasses, as we forgive them that trespass against us*; and has taught us to forgive our Brother, though he offended against us seventy times seven, in Imitation of God's Goodness in forgiving us; and if we must forgive so often, surely God will forgive more than once.

<small>Matt. xviii. 21, 22.</small>

But then Repentance after Baptism requires not only a Sorrow for Sin, and some good Purposes and Resolutions of a new Life for the future, but the actual forsaking of Sin, and Amendment of our Lives: In Baptism God *justifies the ungodly*, Rom. iv. 5. that is, how wicked soever Men have been, whenever they repent of their Sins, renounce their former wicked Practices, and believe in Christ, and enter into Covenant with him by Baptism; all their former Sins are immediately forgiven, are washed away, without expecting the actual Reformation of their Lives. This was plainly the Case both of *Jewish* and *Heathen* Converts, who upon the Profession of Faith in Christ, and renouncing their former wicked Lives, whatever they had been, were immediately received to Baptism; as St. *Peter*

r exhorted the Jews, *Repent,
and be baptized every one of you, in
the name of Jesus Christ, for the remission of sins,
and ye shall receive the gift of the Holy Ghost:
and the same Day there were three thousand
baptized.* This is Gospel-Grace, which is
the Purchase of Christ's Blood, That the
greatest Sinners upon their Repentance and
Faith in Christ, are received to Mercy, and
wash away all their Sins in Baptism. But
when they are in Covenant, they shall then
be judged according to the Terms and Conditions of that Covenant, which requires the
Practice of an universal Righteousness; such
Persons must not expect, as St. *Paul* reasons,
that if they *continue still in sin, grace will
abound*; the very Covenant of Grace, which
we enter into at Baptism, confutes all such
ungodly Hopes. *For how shall we that are
dead to sin, live any longer therein? Know ye
not, that so many of us as were baptized into
Jesus Christ, were baptized into his death?
Therefore we are buried with him by baptism
into Death, that like as Christ was raised from
the dead by the glory of the Father, so we also
should walk in newness of Life,* Rom. vi, 1, 2,
4. This is the Difference St. *Paul* makes
between the Grace of the Gospel in receiving
the greatest Sinners to Baptism, and justifying them by the Blood of Christ; and what
the Gospel requires of baptized Christians to
continue in this justified State: in the first
Case,

Acts ii. 38.

Case, nothing is required but Faith and Repentance, upon which Account we are so frequently said *to be justified by faith, not by the deeds of the law; to be justified freely by his grace, through the redemption that is in Christ Jesus; to be saved by grace through faith; not of works, lest any man should boast.* And I believe upon Enquiry it would be found, that Justification by Faith always relates to this baptismal Justification, when by Baptism we are received into Covenant with God, and into a justified State, only for the Sake of Christ, and through Faith in his Blood. Which one Thing well considered, would put an end to most of the Disputes about Justification, and about Faith and Works. Which I cannot explain now; but shall only observe, that the constant Opposition between Justification by the Faith of Christ, and Justification by Circumcision, and the Works of the Law, to the Observation of which they were obliged by Circumcision, is a manifest Proof that Justification by Faith, is our Justification by the Faith of Christ in Baptism, which is our Admission into the Christian Church, makes us the Members of Christ and the Children of God, which is a State of Grace and Justification; as Circumcision formerly made them God's peculiar People in Covenant with him, which is the Justification of Circumcision: And Justification

Rom. iii. 20. 21, 22, 24.
Rom. v. 1.
Eph. ii. 8; 9.

Gal. v. 2, 3.

tion by Faith, and Justification by Circumcision, would not be duly opposed, if they did not relate to the same Kind of Justification; that is, that Justification which is the immediate Effect of our being in Covenant with God.

But now, when we are justified by a general Repentance and Faith in Christ at Baptism, we also vow a Conformity to the Death of Christ, by *dying to sin, and walking in newness of life*; that is, we vow an universal Obedience to all the Laws of Righteousness, which the Gospel requires of us, as Circumcision made them *debtors to the whole law*, Gal. v. which is the Reason why the Works of the Law, and that evangelical Righteousness which the Faith of Christ requires of us are so often opposed in this Dispute; the one the Righteousness of the Law, or of Works, the other the Righteousness of Faith; and therefore as Circumcision could not justify those who transgressed the Law, no more will Faith justify those who disobey the Gospel; but *the righteousness of the law must be fulfilled in us, who walk not after the flesh but after the spirit*.   Rom. ii. 13, 25, 26, 27, 28, 29. Rom. viii. 4.

Now the necessary Consequence of this is, that mere Sorrow for Sin, and the mere Vows and Resolutions of Obedience, without actual Holiness, and Obedience of Life, according to the Terms and Conditions of the Gospel, will nor live a baptized Christian; for men know [illegible] and Vows of Obedience will be [illegible] only in Baptism; but when we are [illegible] we must put our Vows in Execution [illegible] from our Baptismal Grace and [illegible]. And therefore when we [illegible] after Baptism, no Repentance will be [illegible] but that which actually reforms our Lives, for Baptismal Grace is not [illegible] repeated no more than we can repeat our Baptism.

This I take to be the true Meaning of that severe Place, Heb. vi. 4, 5, 6. *For it is impossible for those who were once enlightened, and have tasted of the heavenly gift, and were made partakers of the Holy Ghost, and have tasted the good word of God and the powers of the world to come, if they shall fall away, to renew them again unto repentance, seeing they crucify to themselves the Son of God afresh, and put him to an open shame.* This severe Passage occasioned some Dispute about the canonical Authority of this Epistle; for it was thought that the Apostle here excluded all Men from the Benefit of Repentance, who fell into Sin again after Baptism; but it is certain this is not the Apostle's Meaning, nor do the Words import any such Doctrine; but his Meaning is, either that Men who have been baptized, and thoroughly instructed in the Christian Religion, may sin themselves into an Impossibility of Repentance, (which is the most ordinary

nary Interpretation of the Words, and which Senfe I gave before of them, and is in part the true Senfe, tho' I think not the whole) or that Men after Baptifm may fall into fuch a State, as nothing can deliver them out of, but baptifmal Grace and Regeneration; and fince Baptifm cannot be repeated, the State of fuch Men is hopelefs and defperate, according to the Terms of the Gofpel, however God may deal with them by a fovereign and prerogative Grace: For though we can expect and rely on no other Grace, but what God has promifed in his Gofpel, yet God does not abfolutely confine himfelf, nor muft we confine his Grace; and this he tells us is the Cafe of all Apoftates from the Chriftian Faith. The underftanding of this is neceffary to my prefent Purpofe; and therefore I fhall briefly explain it:

1. That the Apoftle here fpeaks of Perfons who were baptized, is plain from the Words, *Thofe who were once enlightened*, the ἅπαξ φωτισθέντας, are thofe who have been once baptized; for fo φωτίζειν and φωτισμός in the ancient Writers fignifies Baptifm; as *Juftin Martyr* himfelf tells us in his fecond Apology, that Baptifm is called φωτισμός, or Illumination, becaufe their Minds are enlighten'd by it; and being once enlighten'd, plainly refers it to Baptifm, which can be adminiftred but *once*. And what follows, proves

this to be the Meaning of it; *and have tasted the heavenly gift?* That is, saith St. *Chrysostom*, received Remission of Sins in Baptism; *and were made partakers of the Holy Ghost*, the Holy Spirit being given in Baptism: *And have tasted of the good word of God*, been instructed in the Doctrines of the Gospel, which in the Apostolick Age immediately followed Baptism; for Men were then admitted to Baptism immediately upon their Profession of Repentance and Faith in Christ, and were afterwards instructed in the Christian Religion: *And the powers of the world to come*; that is, those miraculous Gifts and Powers which were bestowed on the Apostles, for a Confirmation of the Faith of Christ, of which most Christians did in some Degree or other partake of in Baptism. This is a plain Description of Baptism, with the Effects and Consequence of it.

2. That he speaks of such as after Baptism totally apostatize from the Faith of Christ, is as plain: For they are παραπεσόντας, *those who fall away.* From what? From their Christian Profession, which they made at their Baptism; that is, who renounce the Faith of Christ, and turn *Jews* or *Heathens* again; for these Men *crucify to themselves the Son of God afresh, and put him to open shame:* That is, they declare him to be an Impostor, as the *Jews* did when they crucified him, which is as

as much crucifying him again, and exposing him to publick Shame and Infamy, as they can possibly do. But now this Description can relate only to total Apostates; for whatsoever Sins professed Christians are guilty of, though thereby they reproach their Lord and Saviour, yet they do not declare him to be an Impostor, who justly suffered on the Cross, and whom they would condemn to the same ignominious Death again if they could; nay, those who are conquered by some powerful and surprizing Fears to deny Christ, as *Peter* did, or to offer Sacrifice to Idols, as many Christians did under the Heathen Persecution, and recover themselves again by Repentance, are not included in this severe Sentence: For such Men do really believe in Christ still, do not heartily renounce their baptismal Faith, and therefore do not lose their Baptism, though in Word and Deed at present they deny Christ. The Case of such Men is very dangerous; for our Saviour tells us, *Whosoever shall deny me before men, him will I also deny before my Father which is in Heaven*, Matth. x. 33. Those who through Fear of Men persist in such a Denial, shall not be saved by a secret and dissembled Faith: for we must not only believe in Christ, but we must openly profess our Faith in him: But such Men may be recovered by Repentance, and by a bold Confession of Christ in new Dangers and Temptations; these are lapsed

lapsed Christians, but not Apostates, as *Julian* was, who hated the Name and Religion of Christ; and therefore they were admitted to Repentance in the Christian Church, as not having lost their baptismal Faith, though through Fear they denied it.

3. Of these total Apostates, the Apostle tells us, That *it is impossible to renew them again unto repentance* ἀνακαινίζειν εἰς μετάνοιαν, or διὰ, as St. *Chrysostom* renders it, to make them new Creatures again by Baptismal Repentance: for so he tells us, that ἀνακαινισθῆναι, καινὸν γενέσθαι, that to be renewed is to be made new, which can be done only by Baptism, τὸ γὰρ καινὸς ποιεῖσθαι τῷ λουτρῷ μόνον ἐςὶ, Baptism only makes us new Creatures.

The Danger then of these Mens Case, as the Apostle represents it, is this: That they having totally apostatized from the Faith of Christ, together with their Faith have lost their Baptism, and are become *Jews* and *Pagans* again: Now *Jews* and *Pagans* can never be made Christians without Baptism, wherein they are regenerated and new made; and by the same Reason these apostatized Christians, who are become *Jews* and *Pagans*, can never become Christians again, unless they be rebaptized; and that they cannot be, because there is but one Baptism in the Christian Church. And therefore, tho' we could suppose, that they should believe again, and repent of their Sins, they could never recover a legal Right and Title to Mercy, and the Promises of the Gospel-Covenant. Faith and Repentance will not justify a Heathen without Baptism; *for he that believes and is baptized shall be saved*, are the express Terms of the Covenant; and therefore the Condition of Apostates is very hopeless, who are relapsed into such a State, that nothing but baptismal Grace and Regeneration, nothing but being new made, and new born, can save them; and that they cannot have, for they must not be baptized again. A Christian must be once born, no more than any Man is, which possibly is the Reason why St. *Peter* tells us of such Apostates, *That their latter end is worse with them than their beginning*, 2 Pet. ii. 20. For *Jews* and *Heathens*, how wicked soever they were, might wash away all their Sins in Baptism; but such Apostates *are like a sow that was washed, that returns again to her wallowing in the mire*. When they had washed away their Sins and Infidelity in Baptism, they return to their forsaken *Paganism* again, and lose the Effect of their first Washing, and there is no second baptismal Washing to be had.

The Apostle does not say, that it is impossible those Men should be saved, but it is impossible they should be regenerated again by Baptism, which is the only Gospel State of Salvation. If any such Men be saved, they must be saved, as I observed before, by uncovenanted Grace and Mercy; they are in the State of unbaptized *Jews* and *Heathens*, not of Christians, who have a Covenant-Right to God's Promises. And I would desire the baptized Atheists and Infidels of our Age to consider of this; whose Case is so very like this, if it be not the same, that it should make them afraid of setting up for Wits, at such infinite Peril of their Souls.

To apply this then to our present Purpose. What I have now discoursed, plainly shews, that a baptized Christian must not always expect to be saved by such Grace as saves and justifies in Baptism: Baptismal Grace is inseparably annexed to Baptism, and can be no more repeated than Baptism. This makes the Case of Apostates so desperate, that Infidelity can be washed away only in Baptism and those who apostatize after Baptism, can never be rebaptized again; and therefore can never have any Covenant-Title to Pardon and Forgiveness.

And this proportionably holds good in our present Case: The Grace of Baptism washes away all the Sins of our past Lives, how many, how great soever they have been, only upon our Profession of our Faith in Christ, and Repentance of all our Sins, and Vows of Obedience to the Laws of Christ for the future: But whoever after Baptism lives a wicked and profligate Life, and hopes to be saved at last only by Faith in Christ, and

Sorrow

Sorrow for his Sins, and Vows of living better when he is juſt a dying, will be miſerably miſtaken; for this is only the Grace of Baptiſm, which can never be repeated, not the Rule and Meaſure whereby God will judge baptized Chriſtians who have had Time and Opportunity of exerciſing thoſe Chriſtian Graces which they vowed at their Baptiſm.

A Man who retains the Faith of Chriſt, though he lives wickedly, does not forfeit his Baptiſm, but ſhall be forgiven whenever he repents, and forſakes his Sins, and lives a holy Life: But if he delays this ſo long, that he has no Time to amend his Life, that he can do nothing but be ſorry for his Sins, and vow a new Life; I cannot promiſe him that this ſhall be accepted at the Hour of Death, becauſe the Goſpel requires a holy Life, not merely a Death-bed Sorrow and Remorſe for Sin. Sorrow for Sin, and Vows of a new Life, will be accepted at Baptiſm, as the Beginnings of a new Life: But that is no Reaſon why they ſhould be accepted at our Death, when they are only the ſorrowful Concluſion of a wicked Life. God will receive us to Grace and Mercy at Baptiſm, upon our ſolemn Vows of living to him; but he has no where promiſed to accept of our dying Vows inſtead of Holineſs and Obedience; as a Recompence for a whole Life ſpent in Wickedneſs and Folly. It is very ſeldom that ſuch dying Sorrows, or dying Vows, are ſincere
and

and hearty; but were they ever so sincere, (as sometimes, tho' very rarely, we see that Men, who recover from a dangerous Sickness, keep the Vows and Promises they then made, and this is a good Proof that they were very sincere in making them) yet do I not know any one Promise in Scripture to a dying Repentance: The Gospel requires actual Holiness of Life; and when God cuts off such Men in their Sins without allowing them any Time to reform their Lives, it is very suspicious that he rejects their Sorrows and their Vows; as Wisdom threatens, Prov. i. 24, &c. *Because I have called, and he refused; I have stretched forth my hand, and no man regarded,——I will laugh also at your calamity, and mock you when fear cometh.——Then shall they call upon me, but I will not answer; they shall seek me early, but they shall not find me.* I will not prejudge the final State of these Men; but if God accept of such a Death-bed Repentance, which cannot produce the actual Fruits of Righteousness, it is more than he has promised, and more than he has given us Authority to preach; and we should consider what infinite Hazard we run by such Delays of Repentance, that we cannot be saved by the express Terms of the Gospel; but if we be saved, we must be saved by an unpromised and uncovenanted Grace and Mercy: Which, how good soever God be, we have no Reason to rely on. This, I know, will be thought very severe, but I cannot help it; it may terrify dying Sinners, but there is less Danger in that than in nursing Men up in the deluding Hopes of a Death-bed Repentance, which renders all the Arguments and Motives to a holy Life ineffectual, and, I fear, eternally destroy, as many as trust in it.

If you ask, why Faith and Repentance, without the actual Obedience of our Lives, should not as well be accepted by God on our Death-bed, as it is at our Baptism? I shall ask another very plain Question, Why a Husbandman who hires Labourers into his Vineyard in the Morning, receives them into his Service, Protection, and Pay, only upon their Promise to be faithful and diligent in his Work before they have done any Thing: I say, when these Men have loitered away the Day without working, why should not he reward them at Night, because they then also profess themselves very sorry that they did not work; and make a great many Promises and Vows; that if they were to begin the Day again they would? A Promise of Faithfulness and Diligence was Reason enough why he should take them into his Service; but their Sorrow for not working, and their Resolutions of working, when the Time of working is past, is no Reason why they should be rewarded, or escape the Punishment of Loiterers.

This

This is the very Case here; we are saved by the Mercies of God, and the Merits of Christ, which we partake of by our Union to him: This Union is made in Baptism, which incorporates us into the Body of Christ; and from the very first Moment of our Union, we are in a State of Grace and Justification; our Sins are washed away in his Blood, as Water purges away all bodily Defilements, and the Spirit of Christ dwells in us to renew and sanctify us: Now all that is required by God, or that seems in the Nature of the Thing necessary to this Union, is a general Repentance of all our Sins, renouncing our former wicked Course of Life, professing our Faith in Christ, as the Son of God, and Saviour of the World, and vowing Obedience to his Laws: for this qualifies us to be his Disciples, and to be received into his Service, and into the Communion of his Body and Church; and therefore this Faith and Repentance justifies in Baptism, because those who thus repent of their Sins, and believe in Christ, are received to Baptism, and in Baptism have all their Sins forgiven, and are put into a State of Grace and Favour with God.

But now tho' Faith and Repentance, and the Vows of Obedience, are sufficient to make us the Disciples of Christ, and to put us into a State of Justification; yet they are not sufficient to save those who are the Disciples of Christ, without actual Holiness and Obedience

dience of Life: For to be a Disciple of Christ does not signify merely to believe in him, and to vow Obedience to him, but to obey him: It is reasonable enough, that upon our Vows of Obedience, we should be received into his Service, but it is not reasonable that we should be rewarded without performing our Vows; for it is as ridiculous a Thing to think that our repeated Sorrows for not obeying, and our repeated and fruitless Resolutions of obeying our Saviour, should pass for Obedience, as that the Son should be thought to do his Father's Will, who said, *I go, Sir*, but went not; especially, when after our Vow of Baptism we live a very ungodly Life, and never think it Time to repent, and to renew our Vows again till we come to die. If we consider the Difference between what is necessary to make us the Disciples of Christ, and what is required of us when we are Disciples, we shall see a plain Reason, why Faith and Repentance, as that signifies Sorrow for Sin, and Vows of Obedience, will justify us in Baptism, and will not be accepted upon a Deathbed, after a Life spent in Wickedness: For when a baptized Christian comes to die, he is not then to be made a Disciple of Christ, and to be baptized again, but to give an Account of his Life since he has been Christ's Disciple; and mere Faith in Christ, Sorrow for Sin, and Vows of Obedience, without actual Holiness of Life, tho' with the Sacrament of Baptism it will make a Disciple, yet it will not paſs in a Diſciple's Account, eſpecially when the ſum Total of his Life is nothing but Sin, and Sorrow, and fruitleſs Vows; for this is not that Holineſs of Life which Chriſt requires of his Diſciples.

The ancient Diſcipline of the Church was a plain Proof of this, that they thought a great deal more neceſſary for a baptized Chriſtian, than was required to qualify Men for Baptiſm. In the Apoſtles Days, they baptized both *Jews* and *Heathens* immediately upon their Profeſſion of Faith in Chriſt, and renouncing their former wicked Lives; but in caſe they fell into any groſs and ſcandalous Sin after Baptiſm, they were caſt out of the Communion of the Church; and the Profeſſion of Sorrow and Repentance for their Sins, and the moſt ſolemn Vows of a new Life, were not thought ſufficient to reſtore them to the Peace of the Church, but they were kept under the Severities of Repentance, till they had made Satisfaction for the Scandal they had given to the Church, and given ſufficient Teſtimonies of the actual Reformation of their Lives. And in the Ages ſucceeding the Apoſtles, this State of Penitence, in ſome Caſes, was continued many Years; in other Caſes, ſuch Sinners were never reconciled to the Hour of Death. Now if they had thought, as many among us now do, that Sorrow for Sin, and the Vows of Obedience, do immediately obtain our Pardon from God, for Sins
committed

mmitted after Baptism, it is not imagina-
 why they should have imposed such a long
d severe Discipline on Penitents. If they
lieved God had forgiven them, Why should
t the Church forgive them, and receive
em to her Communion, again, upon their
omises of Amendment, without such a long
rial of their Reformation? But it is evident,
ey thought Sins after Baptism not forgiven
ithout actual Reformation, and therefore
ɔuld not receive them to Communion again,
ithout a tried and visible Reformation of
eir Lives. We know what Disputes there
ɛre about this Matter in the Primitive
urch; the ancient Discipline allowed but
one Repentance after Baptism: And some
ɔuld not allow of that in the Case of Adul-
·y, Murther, and Idolatry, but denied the
ıthority of the Church to receive such Sin-
rs to Communion again. This was the Pre-
ıce of *Novatus*'s Schism; and *Tertullian*,
er he turned *Montanist*, said many bitter
hings against the Catholicks upon this Ar-
ment, which seemeth to question the Va-
ity of Repentance itself after Baptism, tho'
did reform Mens Lives. But tho' this was
great deal too much, and did both lessen
e Grace of the Gospel, and the Authority
hich Christ hath given to his Church; yet
is evident, that all this Time they were
ry far from thinking that some dying Sor-
ws, or dying Vows after a wicked Life,

would

would carry Men to Heaven: And the Judgment of those first and purest Ages of the Church, ought at least to make Men afraid of relying on such a Death-bed Repentance as they thought very ineffectual to save Sinners.

CHAP. IV.

Concerning the Fear of DEATH, *and the Remedies against it.*

DEATH is commonly and very truly called the King of Terrors, as being the most formidable Thing to human Nature. The Love of Life, and the natural Principle of Self-preservation, begets in all Men a natural Aversion against Death; and this is the natural Fear of dying. This is very much increased by a great Fondness and Passion for this World, which makes such Men, especially while they are happy and prosperous, very unwilling to leave it; and this is still increased by a Sense of Guilt, and the Fear of Punishment in the next World. All these are of a distinct Nature, and require suitable Remedies, and therefore I shall distinctly consider them.

I. The natural Fear of Death results from Self-preservation, and the Love of our own Being: For *light is sweet, and a pleasant thing it is for the Eyes to behold the sun*, Eccl. xi. 7. All Men love Life, and the necessary Consequence of that is, to fear Death; tho' this is rather a natural Instinct, than the Effect of Reason and Discourse.

There are great and wise Reasons why God should imprint this Aversion to Death on human Nature, because it obliges us to take care of ourselves, and to avoid every Thing which will destroy or shorten our Lives: This in many Cases is a great Principle of Virtue, as it preserves us from all fatal and destructive Vices; it is a great Instrument of Government, and makes Men afraid of committing such Villainies as the Laws of their Country have made capital. And therefore, since the natural Fear of Death is of such great Advantage to us, we must be contented with it, though it makes the Thoughts of dying a little uneasy: Especially if we consider, that when this natural Fear of Death is not increased by other Causes, (of which more presently) it may be conquered or allayed by Reason and wise Consideration: For this is not so strong an Aversion, but it may be conquered. The Miseries and Calamities of this Life very often reconcile Men to Death, and make them passionately desire it: *Wherefore is light given to him that is in misery, and life to the bitter in soul? Which long for death, but it cometh not, and dig for it more than for hid treasures; which rejoice exceedingly, and are glad when they can find the grave.*

grave, Job iii. 20, 21, 22. *My soul chuseth strangling, and death rather than life; I loath it, I would not live alway; let me alone, for my days are vanity*, Job vii. 15, 16. And if the Sense of present Sufferings can conquer the Fears of Death, there is no doubt but the Hope of immortal Life may do it also. For the Fear of Death is not an original and primitive Passion, but results from the Love of ourselves, from the Love of our Life, and our own Being; and therefore when we can separate the Fear of Death from Self-love, it is easily conquered. When Men are sensible that Life is no Kindness to them, but only serves to prolong their Misery, they are so far from being afraid of Death, that they court it; and were they as thoroughly convinced, that when they die, Death will translate them to a more happy Life, it would be as easy a Thing to put off these Bodies, as to change their Cloaths, or to leave an old and ruinous House for a more beautiful and convenient Habitation.

If we set aside the natural Aversion, and enquire into the Reasons of this natural Fear of Death, we can think of but these two: Either Men are afraid that when they die they shall cease to be; or at least they know not what they shall be, and are unwilling to change this present Life, which they like very well, for they know not what. But now both these Reasons of Fear are taken away by the Revelation of the Gospel, which has brought Life and nd Immortality to Light; and when the reasons of our Fear are gone, such an unaccountable Aversion and Reluctancy to Death, signifies little more than to make us patient of living, rather than unwilling to die; for a Man who has such a new glorious World, such a happy immortal Life in his View, could not very contentedly delay his Removal thither, were not Death in the Way, which he naturally startles at, and draws back from, though his Reason sees nothing frightful or terrible in it.

The plain and short Account then of this Matter is this: We must not expect wholly to conquer our natural Aversion to Death; St. *Paul* himself did not desire *to be uncloathed, but cloathed upon, that mortality might be swallowed up of life*, 2 Cor. iii. 4. Were there not some remaining Aversions to Death mixed with our Hopes and Desires of Immortality, Martyrdom itself, excepting the patient enduring the Shame and Torments of it, would be no Virtue. But tho' this natural Aversion to Death cannot be wholly conquered, it may be extremely lessened, and brought next to nothing, by the certain Belief and Expectation of a glorious Immortality; and therefore the only Way to arm ourselves against these natural Fears of dying, is to confirm ourselves in this Belief, that Death does not put an End to us, that our Souls shall live in a State of Bliss and Happiness, when our Bodies shall rot in their Graves,

T 2 and

and that these mortal Bodies themselves shall at the Sound of the last Trump rise again out of the Dust immortal and glorious. A Man who believes and expects this, can have no Reason to be afraid of Death; nay, he has great Reason not to fear Death, and that will reconcile him to the Thoughts of it, though he trembles a little under the Weakness and Aversions of Nature.

II. Besides the natural Aversions to Death, most Men have contracted a great Fondness and Passion for this World, and that makes them so unwilling to leave it. Whatever glorious Things they hear of another World, they see what is to be had in this, and they like it so well, that they do not expect to mend themselves, but if they were at their Choice, would stay where they are; and this is a double Death to them, to be snatch'd away from their admired Enjoyments, and to leave whatever they love and delight in behind them; and there is no Remedy that I know of for these Men to cure their Fears of Death, but only to rectify their mistaken Opinion of Things, to open their Eyes to see the Vanity of this World, and the brighter and more dazling Glories of the next.

There are different Degrees of this, and therefore this Remedy must be differently applied: Some Men are wholly sunk into Flesh and Sense, and have no Taste at all of rational and manly Pleasures, much less of those

those which are purely intellectual and divine; they are Slaves to their Lusts, and lay no Restraints on their brutish Appetites; the World is their God, and they dote on the Riches, and Pleasures, and Honours of it, as the only real and substantial Goods: Now these Men have great Reason to be afraid of Death; for when they go out of this World, they will find nothing that belongs to this World in the next; and thus their Happiness and their Lives must end together: It is fitting they should fear Death, for if the Fear of Death will not cure their Fondness for this World, nothing else can; you must not expect to persuade them that the next World is a happier Place than this: But the best Way is to set before them the Terrors of the next World, those Lakes of Fire and Brimstone prepared for the Devil and his Angels; to ask them our Saviour's Question, *What shall it profit a man to gain the whole world, and to lose his own soul; or what shall a man give in exchange for his soul?* These Men ought to fear on 'till the Fear of Death cures their vicious Passion and Fondness for this World, and then the Fear of Death will by degrees cure itself.

Others there are who have a true Reverence for God, and govern their Inclinations and Passions to the Things of this World, with regard to his Laws; they will not raise an Estate by Injustice, Oppression, or Perjury; they will not transgress the Rules of Sobriety and Modesty in the Use of sensual Pleasures;

they will not purchase the Honours and Preferments of this World at the Price of their Souls; but yet they love this World very well, and are extremely delighted in the Enjoyments of it; they have a plentiful Fortune, or a thriving Trade, or the Favour of their Prince: They live at Ease, and think this World a very pleasant Place, and are ready to cry, *It is good for us to be here.* Now it cannot be avoided, but that in Proportion to Mens Love for this World, though it be not an immoral and irregular Passion, they will be more afraid, and more unwilling to leave it. When we are in the full Enjoyment of an earthly Felicity, it is difficult for very good Men to have such a strong and vigorous Sense of the next World, as to make them willing and contented to leave this; they desire to go to Heaven, but they are not overhasty in their Desires; they can be better pleased, if God sees fit, to stay here a little longer; and when they find themselves a going, are apt to cast back their Eyes upon this World, as those who are loth to part. This makes it so necessary for God to exercise even good Men with Afflictions and Sufferings, to wean them from this World, which is a Scene of Misery, and to raise their Hearts to Heaven, where true and unmixed Happiness dwells.

The only Way then to cure this Fear of Death, is to mortify all Remains of Love, and Affection for this World; to withdraw ourselves as much as may be from the Conversation erfation of it; to use it very sparingly, and with great Indifferency; to supply the Wants of Nature, rather than to enjoy the Pleasures of it; to have our Conversation in Heaven, to meditate on the Glories of that blessed Place; to live in this World upon the Hopes of unseen Things; to accustom ourselves to the Work and to the Pleasures of Heaven, to praise and adore the great Maker and Redeemer of the World, to mingle ourselves with the heavenly Choir, and possess our very Fancies and Imaginations with the Glory and Happiness of seeing GOD and the blessed JESUS, of dwelling in his immediate Presence, of conversing with Saints and Angels. This is to live like Strangers in this World, and like Citizens of Heaven; and then it will be as easy to us to leave this World for Heaven, as it is for a Traveller to leave a foreign Country to return Home. This is the Height and Perfection of Christian Virtue; it is our mortifying the Flesh with it's Affections and Lusts; it is our dying to this World, and living to God; and when we are dead to this World, the Fear of dying and leaving this World is over: For what should a Man do in this World, who is dead to it? When we are alive to God, nothing can be so desirable as to go to him: for here we live to God only by Faith and Hope, but that is the proper Place for this divine Life, where God dwells: So that, in short, a Life of Faith as is our Victory over the World, so it is our

T 4 Victory

Victory over Death too; it difarms it of all it's Fears and Terrors; it raifes our Hearts fo much above this World, that we are very well pleafed to get rid of thefe Bodies which keep us here, and to leave them in the Grave, in Hopes of a bleffed Refurrection.

III. The moft tormenting Fears of Death are owing to a Senfe of Guilt, which indeed are rather a Fear of Judgment than of Death, or a Fear of Death, as it fends us to Judgment: And here we muft diftinguifh between three Sorts of Men whofe Cafe is very different; 1. Thofe who are very good Men, who have made the Care of their Lives to pleafe God, and fave their Souls. 2. Thofe who have lived very ungodly Lives, and are now awakened by the Approaches of Death, to fee an angry and provoked Judge, an injured Saviour, a righteous Tribunal, and think they hear that fatal Doom and Sentence pronounced on them by their own Confciences, *Go ye curfed into everlafting fire, prepared for the devil and his angels.* 3. Thofe who are doubtful of their own Condition, and are apt to fear the worft.

1. As for the firft Sort of thefe Men, who have fincerely endeavoured to pleafe GOD, and have the Teftimony of their Confciences, that in Simplicity and godly Sincerity, they have had their Converfation in this World, Chrift has delivered them from all their Fears by his Death upon the Crofs, and his Interceffion

cession for them at the Right-Hand of God: The best Men dare not stand the Trial of strict and impartial Justice; they are conscious to themselves of so many Sins, of such great Imperfections and Defects, that their only Hope is in the Mercy of God, thro' the Merits and Mediation of Christ; and in this Hope they can triumph over Death, as St. *Paul* does; *O death! where is thy sting? O grave! where is thy victory? The sting of death is sin, and the strength of sin is the law*; but thanks be to God *who hath given us the victory through our Lord Jesus Christ*; who destroyed Sin, and plucked out the Sting of Death by his Death upon the Cross; who triumphed over Death by his Resurrection from the Dead, and is invested with Power to raise all his true Disciples from the Dead: *Is able to save to the utmost, all those that come unto God by him, seeing he ever liveth to make intercession for them.*

1 Cor. xv. 55, 56, 57.

Heb. vii. 25.

This is the happy State of good Men, when they come to die, they can look into the other World without Terror, where they see, not a Court of Justice, but a Throne of Grace; where they see a Father, not a Judge; a Saviour who died for them, and has redeemed them with his own Blood: What a blessed Calm and Serenity possesses their Souls! Nay, what Joy and Triumph transports them! How *do their souls magnify the Lord, and their spirits rejoice in God their Saviour*; when they see him ready to pronounce them blessed, and to set the Crown upon their Heads! Who would not *die the death of the righteous, and desire that his latter end may be like his?* What wise Man would not live the Life of the Righteous, *that his latter end may be like his?* That in the Agonies of Death, and in the very Jaws of the Grave, no disturbed Thoughts may discompose him, no guilty Fears distract him, but he may go out of the World with all the joyful Presages of Eternal Rest and Peace?

2. As for wicked Men, who never concerned themselves with the Thoughts of God and another World, while they were in Health, many times a dangerous Sickness, which gives them a nearer View of Death and Judgment, awakens their Consciences, and overwhelms them with the unsupportable Terrors of future Vengeance; then they begin to lament their ill-spent Lives, to tremble before the just and righteous Judge, whom they have provoked by repeated Villainies: whose Being they formerly denied, or whose Power and Justice they defied; now they cry passionately to Christ for Mercy, and will needs have him to be their Saviour, tho' they would not own him for their Lord, nor submit to his Laws and Government; now these Men are mighty earnest for Comfort; the Minister, who was the Subject of their Drollery before, is sent for in great haste, and it is expected from him that he should lull their Consciences

sciences asleep, and send them quietly into another World to receive their Doom there.

Now it is very fitting to let these Men know, while they are well, that there is no Comfort to be had when they come to die: *For there is no peace, saith my GOD, to the wicked:* And no Man who knows them, can speak Peace to them, without making a new Gospel, or corrupting the old one.

What I have already discoursed concerning a Death-bed Repentance, is a plain Proof of this: But tho' we set aside all that, and proceed upon the common Principle, That a true Penitent, whenever he sincerely repents, tho' it be upon his Death-bed, after a long Life of Wickedness, shall be pardoned and rewarded by God: Yet upon these Principles it is impossible that a wicked Man, when he comes to die, should have any Comfort, without a vain and enthusiastick Presumption; and the Reason is very plain, because it is impossible, either for himself or others to judge, whether his Repentance be true and sincere; such a Repentance, as if he was to live longer, would reform his Life, and bring forth the Fruits of an universal Righteousness: And it is agreed on all Hands, that no other Repentance but this, can be accepted by God.

Now it is absolutely impossible, without a Revelation, for any Man to know this, who begins his Repentance upon a Death-bed: He may feel indeed the bitter Pangs and Agonies of Sorrow, and may be sincerely and

heartily

heartily sorry that he has sinned. And this every dying Sinner is, who is sorrowful: He is sincerely sorrowful; that is, he does not counterfeit a Sorrow, but really feels it. And I know nothing else to make Sorrow sincere, but that it is real, and not counterfeited; and therefore to be sorrowful, and to be sincerely sorrowful, is the same Thing. And will any Man say, that whoever is sorry for his Sins, when he comes to die, shall be saved? Then no Sinner can be damned who does not die an Atheist, or stupid and distracted, or suddenly without any Warning: For it is impossible for a Sinner who is in his Wits, and believes that wicked Men shall be eternally punished in the next World, not to feel an amazing Remorse and Sorrow of Mind, when he sees himself just a falling into Hell.

A dying Sorrow then, though it may be sharp and severe, almost to the Degree of Amazement and Distraction, (and it is hard if such a Sorrow be not real and sincere) is not saving Repentance; and therefore though Sinners may feel themselves very heartily sorrowful, this does not prove them to be true Penitents: And yet this is the only Evidence they can have of their Repentance, and the only thing they can rely on, that they are sure their Sorrow is very sincere: And I doubt not but it is, for all true Sorrow is sincere; but Sinners, who are very sorry for their Sins, may be damned.

Since

Since then Sorrow for Sin is the only Evidence such Men can have of the Sincerity of their Repentance, let us consider, whether the mere dying Sorrows of Sinners be any Evidence at all of this, or what kind of Evidence it is.

True Repentance does at least include a Change of Mind, a turning from our Sins to God, a deep Sense of the Evil of Sin, and an Abhorrence of ourselves for it; a great Reverence for God, and for his Laws, as well as Dread of his Judgments; and deliberate and serious Resolutions of changing our Course of Life, and for the Time to come, of living to God, and to the Purposes of his Glory, never to return to our old Sins again, but diligently to exercise ourselves in all the Duties and Offices of a Christian Life.

Now, suppose a Man who has lived wickedly all his Life, should be thus changed in a Moment, and prove such a true Penitent as I have now described; and that God, who knows the Hearts of Men, sees that his Promises and Vows are sincere, and that if he were to live any longer, he would be a good Man, and therefore will pardon and reward him, not according to what he has done, but according to what he foresees he would have done, had he lived any longer; (which is to judge Men, not according to their Works, but according to his own Fore knowledge, which the Scripture never makes the Rule of future Judgment) I say, suppose such Men

may

may be true Penitents, and pardoned by God, who knows that they are so; yet they can never have the Comfort of it before they die, because it is impossible for them to know it.

When Men see themselves a dying, they are very sorrowful for their Sins, so they say; But the most likely Account of it is, that they are very sorry that they are going to Hell as a Malefactor is very sorrowful when he is going to a Gibbet. This may be the whole of their Sorrow; and it is impossible to prove that there should be any thing more in it, and extremely improbable that there is. For what likelihood is there, that Men, who Yesterday were very much in Love with their Sins, and as little thought of falling out with them, as they did of their dying Day, should To-day, as soon as ever they are arrested with a threatning Sickness, be Penitents in good earnest, and abhor their Sins in a Minute, and be quite other Men upon the View of the other World? This is the Case of all Sinners when they come to die; which makes it very suspicious that there is nothing extraordinary in it, no miraculous Power of the divine Spirit to change their Hearts in a Moment, and make them new Men, but only the common Effect of a great Fear, which makes Men sorry for their Sins, when they come to suffer for them.

Now if such dying Sinners can never be sure, that their Sorrow for Sin is any thing more than a great Fright, they can be sure of nothing else; for such a Sorrow as this will counter-

counterfeit all the other Acts of Repentance. Men who are terribly afraid of Punishment, are not only sorry for their Sins, but this very Sorrow makes them ashamed of them, gives them a great Indignation against themselves for them, makes them flatter their Judge, and vow and promise Reformation if they could escape this one time. And this is so very common and familiar, that in all other Cases no Man regards it: A Judge, a Father, or a Master, will not spare upon such Promises as these; and why should this be thought any thing more in a dying Sinner, than in other Malefactors? Why should that be thought a sufficient Reason for God to pardon, which we ourselves think no Reason in all other Cases? All this may be no more than the Fear of Hell; and I doubt the mere Fear of Hell when Men are a dying, tho' it may imitate all the Scenes of Repentance, will not keep them out of Hell. It is so very probable, that this is the whole of a Death-bed Repentance, that no such dying Sinner can have any reasonable Hope that he does truly repent; and therefore, unless he flatter himself when he dies, with a false and counterfeit Repentance, as he did while he lived, with the Hope of repenting before he died, he must expire in all the Terrors and Agonies of guilty Fears. This is so miserable a Condition, that tho' we should suppose such a Sinner may be a true Penitent, and go to Heaven at last, yet no wise Man would endure these dying

Agonies

Agonies for all the false and deceitful Pleasures of Sin: And yet there is no possible Way of avoiding this, but by such a timely Repentance while we are well, and Death at a Distance, as may bring forth the actual Fruits of Holiness, that when we come to die, we may have some better Evidence of the Sincerity of our Repentance, than mere dying Sorrows.

3. Let us now consider the Case of those who are doubtful what their Condition is; who are neither so good as to be out of all Danger and Fear, nor so bad as to be out of Hope: And I need not tell any Man that this is a State between Hope and Fear, which is a very uneasy State, when eternal Happiness or Misery is the Matter of the Doubt. This is the Case of those Men, who after all their good Resolutions, are ever and anon conquered by Temptations; who as soon as their Tears are dried up for their last Fall, fall again, and then lament their Sins, and resolve again; and while they are thus interchangeably sinning, repenting, and resolving, before they have got a lasting Victory, or are arrived to a steady Virtue, are summon'd by Death to Judgment; or those who have a Reverence for God, but are not so constant and frequent in their Devotions; or if they abstain from gross and scandalous Vices, yet they have not a due Government of their Passions, or do very little Good in the World, &c. Here is such a Mixture of Good and Evil, that it is hard to know which is predominant: While

such Men are in Health, they are very uneasy, and know not what to judge of themselves; but they fall into much greater Perplexities, when they are alarmed with the near Approaches of Death and Judgment. And what a deplorable State is this, when we are a dying, to be uncertain and anxious what will become of us to Eternity?

Now there is no possible Way to prevent these Fears when we come to die, but by giving all Diligence to make our Calling and Election sure, by living such holy and innocent Lives, that our Consciences may not condemn us; and then we shall have Confidence towards God. 1 John iii. 20, 21.

But this is such a Remedy, as few of these Men like: They would be glad to be sure of Heaven, but yet would go as near Hell as they can, without Danger of falling into it; they will serve God, but must reserve a little Favour and Indulgence to their Lusts; tho' they dare not take full Draughts of sensual Pleasures, yet they must be sipping now and then, as often as they can pacify their Consciences, and get rid of the Fear of God, and of another World; and therefore they are very inquisitive after other Cures for an accusing and condemning Conscience; are mighty fond of such Marks and Signs of Grace, as will secure them of Heaven, without the Severities of Mortification, or the constant and uniform Practice of an universal Righteousness: And a great many such Signs have been invented, which like strong Opiates asswage their Pain and Smart, 'till their Consciences awake when it is too late in the next World.

For all this is Cheat and Delusion, as St. *John* assures us, *Little Children, Let no man deceive you; he that doth righteousness is righteous, even as he is righteous. He that committeth sin, is of the devil, for the devil sinneth from the beginning: For this purpose the Son of God was manifested, that he might destroy the works of the devil. Whosoever is born of God, doth not commit sin; for his seed remaineth in him, and he cannot sin, because he is born of God. In this the children of God are manifest, and the children of the devil; whosoever doth not righteousness is not of God, neither he that loveth not his brother.* This is the only sure Evidence for Heaven; and therefore every Sin Men commit, makes their State doubtful, and this must fill them with Perplexities and Fears: Men may cheat themselves with vain Hopes and Imaginations when they come to die; but nothing can be a solid Foundation for Peace and Security, but an universal Righteousness.

1 John. iii. 7, 8, 9, 10.

The Conclusion.

FOR the Conclusion of this Discourse, I shall only observe in a few Words, That it must be the Business of our whole Lives to prepare for Death: Our Accounts must be always ready, because we know not how soon we may be called to give an Account of our Stewardship; we must be always upon our Watch, as not knowing what Hour our Lord will come. A good Man, who has taken care all his Life to please God, has little more to do when he sees Death approaching, than to take leave of his Friends, to bless his Children, to support and comfort himself with the Hopes of immortal Life, and a glorious Resurrection, and to resign up his Spirit into the Hands of God and of his Saviour: His Lamp is full of Oil, and always burning, tho' it may need a little Trimming when the Bridegroom comes; some few Acts of Faith and Hope, *Matth.* xxv. 1, *&c.* and such devout Passions as are proper to be exercised at our leaving the World, and going to God: But when the Bridegroom is at the Door, it is too late with the foolish Virgins to buy Oil for our Lamps: Unless we be ready when the Bridegroom comes, to enter in with him to the Marriage, the Door will be shut against us; *Watch therefore, for ye know neither the day nor the hour wherein the Son of man cometh.*

Some Men talk of preparing for Death, as if it were a thing that could be done in two or three Days, and that the proper Time of doing it were a little before they die; but I know no other Preparation for Death but living well: And thus we must every Day prepare for Death, and then we shall be well prepared when Death comes; that is, we shall be able to give a good Account of our Lives, and of the Improvement of our Talents; and he who can do this, is well prepared to die, and to go to Judgment; but he who has spent all his Days wickedly, whatever Care he may take when he comes to die, to prepare himself for it, it is certain he can never prepare a good Account of his past Life, and all his other Preparations are little worth.

The END.

SD - #0090 - 040324 - C0 - 229/152/16 - PB - 9780259201533 - Gloss Lamination